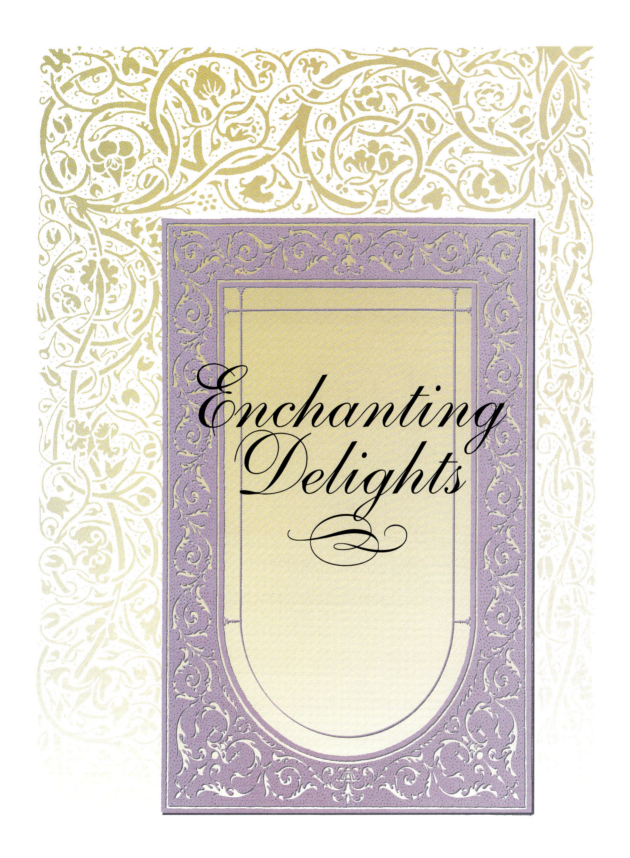

Enchanting Delights

Editorial Director: DONNA ROBERTSON
Design Director: FRAN ROHUS
Production & Photography Director:
ANGE VAN ARMAN

EDITORIAL
Senior Editor: NANCY HARRIS
Editor: MARYLEE KLINKHAMMER
Assistant Editor: REBECCA BIRCH MOEHNKE
Copy Editor/Proofreader: SALWAY SABRI

PRODUCTION
Book Design: GREG SMITH
Production Manager: JEAN SCHRECENGOST
Color Specialist: BETTY RADLA
Production Coordinator: GLENDA CHAMBERLAIN

PHOTOGRAPHY
Photography Manager:
SCOTT CAMPBELL
Photographers:
RUSSELL CHAFFIN, KEITH GODFREY
Photography Coordinator/Stylist:
RUTH WHITAKER

PRODUCT DESIGN
Design Coordinator: TONYA FLYNN

BUSINESS
C.E.O: JOHN ROBINSON
Vice President/Marketing: GREG DEILY

CREDITS
Sincerest thanks to all the designers, manufacturers and other professionals whose dedication has made this book possible.

Copyright © 1998 The Needlecraft Shop, LLC

All rights reserved. No part of this book may be reproduced in any form or by any means without the written permission of the publisher, excepting brief quotations in connection with reviews written specifically for inclusion in magazines, newspapers and other publications.
Library of Congress Cataloging-in-Publication Data
ISBN: 1-57367-105-3
First Printing: 1998
Library of Congress Catalog Card Number: 98-66976
Published and Distributed by
The Needlecraft Shop, LLC, Big Sandy, Texas 75755
Printed in the United States of America.

Contents

Wonders of Friendship
Sweet Friendships 54
To Have Friends 56
Fishing Buddies 60
Rose Heart 63
Best Friends 66
A True Friend 68
A Mother's Love 70

Home Cooked Kindness
Happy Home Recipe 8
Basket of Apples 11
Kitty With Flowers 14
Garden Kitchen Set 17
Pastry Shop 20
Teacups 24

Gardens for the Heart
Beauty Blooms 74
Indigo 77
Perfect Pansies 80
Spring Bouquets 83
For Wrent 86
Plant a Garden 88
God's Garden 91
Garden Alphabet 94

Elegant Magical Touches
Seasonal Birds 28
Unicorn Sampler 32
Old Fashioned Flower Basket . 35
Orchid & Butterfly 38
Circle of Roses 40
Marriage Sampler 44
Enchanted Castle 48

Blessings From Above

Believing 98
Let Love 102
Simple Pleasures 104
First of May 106
Help Me Remember 110
Consider the Birds 113
Advice to the Graduate 116

The Splendor of Christmas

Angels 122
Holiday Trims 126
Elegant Ornaments 129
Country Ornaments 132
Christmas Bear 135
Santa's Cat 138
Santa 142
Mr. Snowman 146
Flying Angel 149

General Instructions

Tools of the Stitcher 152
Stitching Threads 153
Before You Begin 154
Stitching Techniques 155
Cleaning Your Needlework 156
Framing & Mounting 157
Stitch Guide 158
Acknowledgments 159
Index 160

Home Cooked Kindness

Enchanting Delights

Chapter One

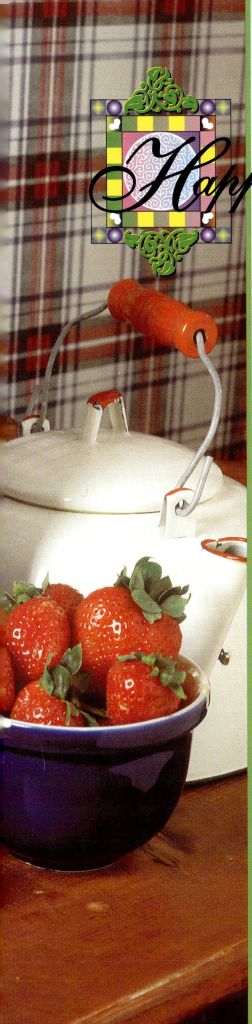

Happy Home Recipe

Designed by Kathleen Hurley

Materials

- 14" x 15" piece of cornflower blue 14-count Aida

Stitch Count:
124 wide x 104 high

Approximate Design Size:
11-count 11 3/8" x 9 1/2"
14-count 8 7/8" x 7 1/2"
16-count 7 3/4" x 6 1/2"
18-count 7" x 5 7/8"
22-count 5 5/8" x 4 3/4"

Instructions

Select desired letters and numbers from Alphabet & Numbers graph, center and stitch design, using two strands floss for Cross-Stitch and Backstitch of lettering and tendrils. Use one strand floss for remaining Backstitch and French Knot.

Alphabet & Numbers

X	B'st	1/4x	Fr	DMC	ANCHOR	J.&P. COATS	COLORS
			●	#310	#403	#8403	Black
■		◪		#498	#1005	#3000	Garnet
▣				#666	#46	#3046	Geranium Dk.
▪				#762	#234	#8510	Silver Very Lt.
▦	◪	▦		#798	#131	#7022	Blueberry Dk.
■		◪		#905	#257	#6258	Parrot Green Dk.
▫	◪	▫		#907	#255	#6001	Parrot Green Lt.
			●	#972	#298	#2298	Tangerine Med.
▨		▨		#973	#297	#2290	Lemon
□		□		White	#2	#1001	White

9

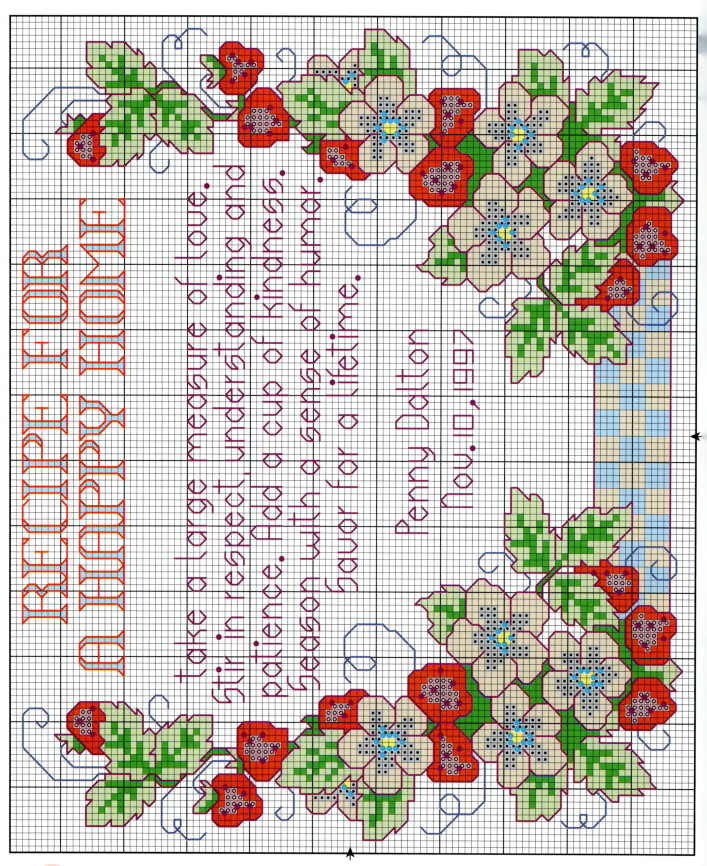

Basket of Apples

Photo on Page 11

Stitch Count:
119 wide x 96 high

Approximate Design Size:
11-count 10⅞" x 8¾"
14-count 8½" x 6⅞"
16-count 7½" x 6"
18-count 6⅝" x 5⅜"
22-count 5½" x 4⅜"

Materials

- 13" x 15" piece of ivory 14-count Aida

Instructions

Center and stitch design, using three strands floss or two strands floss as indicated on color key for Cross-Stitch. Use one strand floss or two strands floss as indicated on color key for Backstitch. Use three strands floss for Straight Stitch and French Knot. Use two strands floss for Lazy Daisy Stitch.

*A scent of ripeness from over a wall.
And come to leave the routine road
And look for what had made me stall,
There sure enough was an appletree
That had eased itself of its summer load,
And of all but its trivial foliage free, …*

*From "Unharvested"
by Robert Frost*

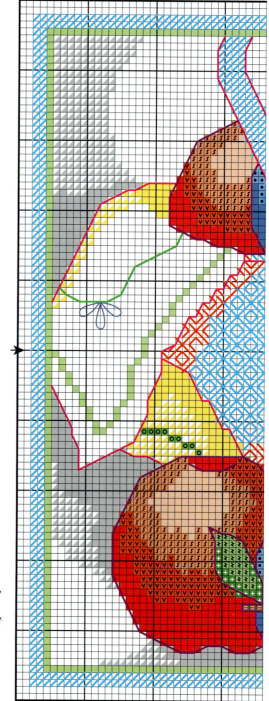

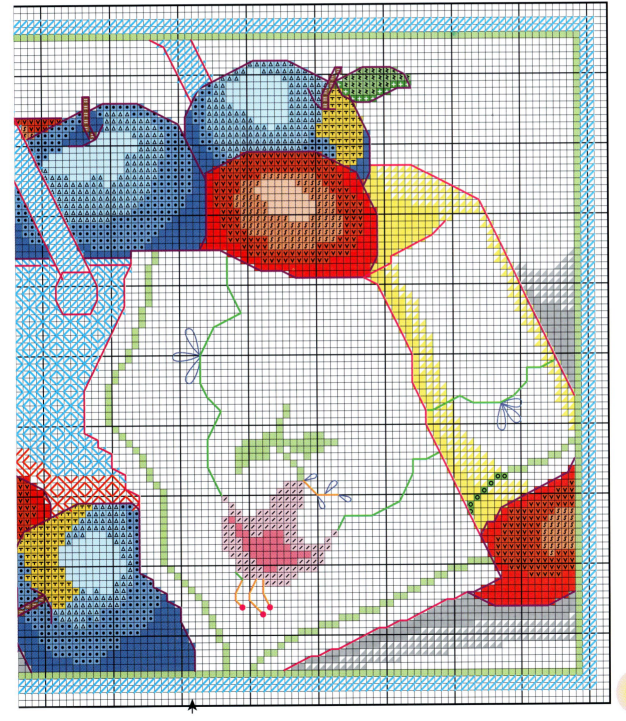

Kitty With Flowers
Designed by Kathleen Hurley

Materials

- 16" x 16" piece of white 28-count Lugana®

Instructions

Center and stitch design, stitching over two threads and using two strands floss for Cross-Stitch and one strand floss for Backstitch, Straight Stitch and Lazy Daisy Stitch.

Stitch Count:
142 wide x 144 high

Approximate Design Size:
11-count 13" x 13 1/8"
14-count 10 1/4" x 10 3/8"
16-count 8 7/8" x 9"
18-count 8" x 8"
22-count 6 1/2" x 6 5/8"
28-count over two threads 10 1/4" x 10 3/8"

X	B'st	1/4x	Str	LzD	DMC	ANCHOR	J.&P. COATS	COLORS
	/		/		#310	#403	#8403	Black
					#319	#218	#6246	Spruce
					#320	#215	#6017	Pistachio Green Med.
	/				#335	#38	#3283	Rose Pink Dk.
					#368	#214	#6016	Pistachio Green Lt.
					#414	#235	#8513	Silver Dk.
					#415	#398	#8398	Silver
					#433	#358	#5471	Coffee Brown
					#444	#290	#2290	Lemon Dk.
					#543	#933	#5533	Bone
					#553	#98	#4097	Violet Med.
					#554	#96	#4104	Violet Lt.
					#720	#326	#2322	Orange Spice Dk.
					#722	#323	#2323	Orange Spice Lt.
					#738	#361	#5375	Toast Very Lt.
					#760	#1022	#3069	Salmon
					#761	#1021	#3068	Salmon Lt.
	/				#842	#368	#5933	Pecan Cream
					#930	#1035	#7052	Blue Denim Dk.
					#931	#1034	#7051	Blue Denim Med.
					#932	#1033	#7050	Blue Denim Lt.
					#972	#298	#2298	Tangerine Med.
					#975	#355	#5356	Cinnamon Dk.
					#976	#1001	#2308	Golden Brown Med.
					#3012	#844	#6844	Olive Green
					#3326	#36	#3126	Rose Pink
					#3328	#1024	#3071	Salmon Dk.
					#3347	#266	#6010	Ivy Green
					#3348	#264	#6266	Apple Green
					#3687	#68	#3088	Mauve Med.
					#3688	#66	#3087	Mauve
					White	#2	#1001	White

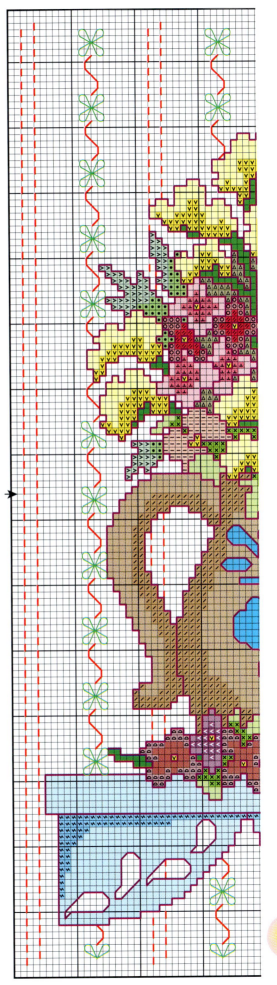

Garden Kitchen Set
Designed by Mike Vickery

Garden Kitchen Set

PHOTO ON PAGE 17

Materials

- Ecru pot holder with 5" x 7" 14-count Aida pocket
- 15" x 25" ecru huck towel with 3" 14-count Aida insert

Instructions

Center and stitch "Pot Holder" design onto pot holder insert and "Towel" design onto towel insert, using two strands floss for Cross-Stitch and one strand floss for Backstitch.

Pot Holder Stitch Count: 75 wide x 59 high

Approximate Design Size:
11-count 6⅞" x 5⅜"
14-count 5⅜" x 4¼"
16-count 4¾" x 3¾"
18-count 4¼" x 3⅜"
22-count 3½" x 2¾"

Towel Stitch Count: 148 wide x 20 high

Approximate Design Size:
11-count 13½" x 1⅞"
14-count 10⅝" x 1½"
16-count 9¼" x 1¼"
18-count 8¼" x 1⅛"
22-count 6¾" x 1"

X	B'st	DMC	ANCHOR	J.&P. COATS	COLORS
■		#498	#1005	#3000	Garnet
■		#550	#102	#4107	Darkest Amethyst
S		#552	#99	#4092	Violet Dk.
△		#553	#98	#4097	Violet Med.
■		#554	#96	#4104	Violet Lt.
ℨ		#644	#830	#5830	Beige Grey Lt.
●		#666	#46	#3046	Geranium Dk.
■		#700	#229	#6227	Kelly Green
O		#702	#227	#6239	Kelly Green Lt.
■		#704	#225	#6238	Parrot Green Med.
T		#822	#390	#5933	Beige Grey Very Lt.
■		#904	#258	#6258	Darkest Parrot Green
V		#906	#256	#6256	Parrot Green Med. Dk.
■		#907	#255	#6001	Parrot Green Lt.
■		#3345	#268	#6269	Ivy Green Dk.
⁄		#3347	#266	#6010	Ivy Green
■		#3348	#264	#6266	Apple Green
⌀		#3705	#35	#3012	Carnation Dk.
■		#3708	#31	#3125	Carnation Lt.
	⁄	#3799	#236	#8999	Charcoal Dk.
■		White	#2	#1001	White

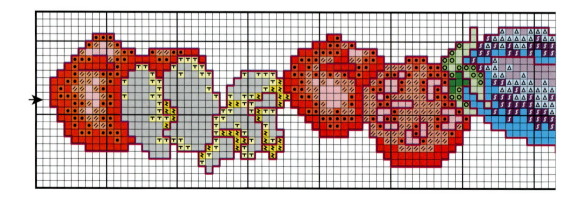

Pot Holder

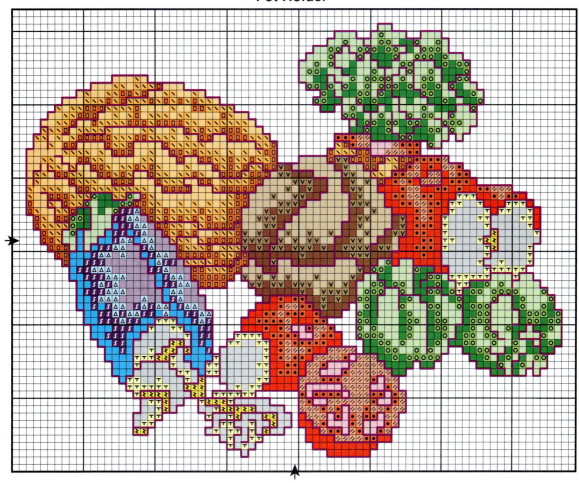

Towel

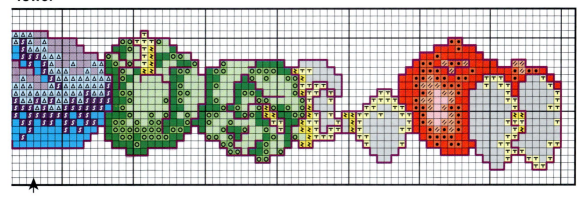

Pastry Shop

Designed by Barbara Smith

Materials

- 15" x 18" piece of ivory 14-count Aida

Stitch Count:
120 wide x 160 high

Approximate Design Size:
11-count 11" x 14⅝"
14-count 8⅝" x 11½"
16-count 7½" x 10"
18-count 6¾" x 9"
22-count 5½" x 7⅜"

Instructions

Center and stitch design, using two strands floss for Cross-Stitch. Use one strand floss or two strands floss as indicated on color key for Backstitch. Use one strand floss for Straight Stitch and French Knot.

Breathe deep, what do you smell?
I know that aroma,
I know it well.
I wait with anticipation,
And I'm first in line.
I've got plate and my knife,
And butter on the side.
I know it's coming shortly,
Lord, I can hardly wait,
There's nothing like fresh homemade bread,
Especially when it's on "my" plate!
Yum. Yum.

From " Grandma's Hearth "
by Jannie Birch

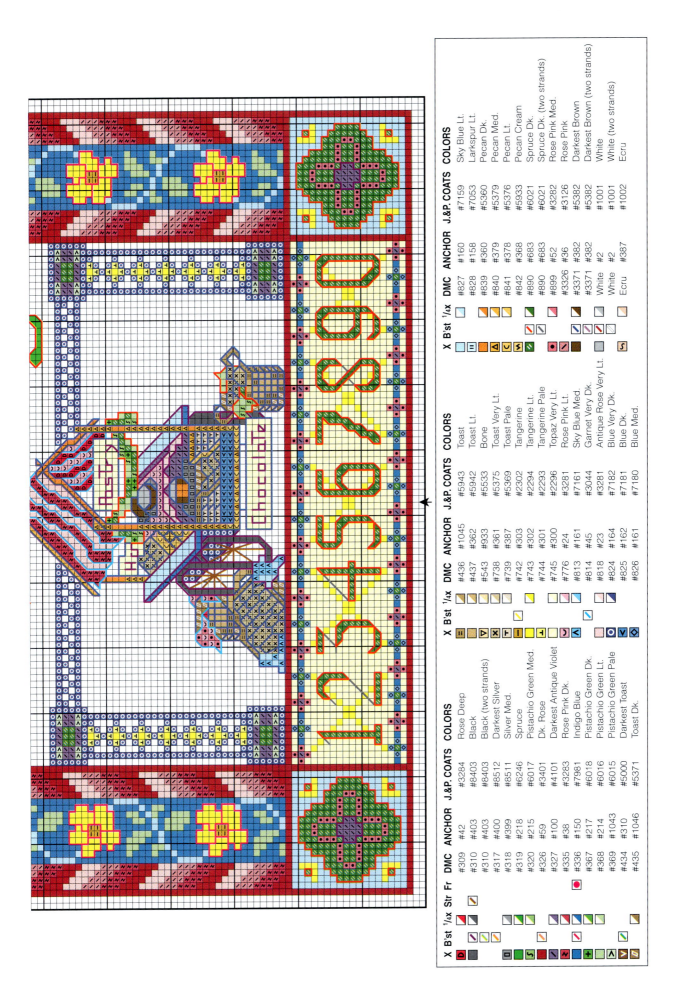

Materials

- 10" x 18" piece of sky blue 28-count Linen
- 9" x 19" wooden shelf
- 5½" x 14½" piece of mounting board
- 8½" x 17½" piece of fabric
- 1⅛ yds. decorative lace
- ¼ yd. ¼" ribbon
- Craft glue or glue gun

Instructions

1: Center and stitch design, stitching over two threads and using two strands floss for Cross-Stitch and one strand floss for Backstitch.

Note: Trim design to 5" x 13¾".

2: Press design edges under ¼". Sew lace to back outside edges of design.

3: Cover mounting board with fabric; center and glue design to covered board.

4: Center and glue covered board to wooden shelf as shown in photo. Tie ribbon into a bow; glue to corner of design as shown.

Stitch Count:
173 wide x 53 high

Approximate Design Size:
- 11-count 15¾" x 4⅞"
- 14-count 12⅜" x 3⅞"
- 16-count 10⅞" x 3⅜"
- 18-count 9⅝" x 3"
- 22-count 7⅞" x 2½"
- 28-count over two threads 12⅜" x 3⅞"

X	DMC	ANCHOR	J.&P. COATS	COLORS	X B'st	DMC	ANCHOR	J.&P. COATS	COLORS
⊙	#318	#399	#8511	Silver Med.		#712	#926	#1002	Cream Very Pale
+	#350	#11	#3111	Coral Med.		#725	#305	#2294	Topaz Med.
	#352	#9	#3008	Peach Flesh Dk.	S	#727	#293	#2289	Topaz Lt.
D	#353	#8	#3006	Peach Flesh Med.	•	#739	#387	#5369	Toast Pale
	#433	#358	#5471	Coffee Brown	II	#746	#275	#2275	Honey Pale
	#435	#1046	#5371	Toast Dk.		#776	#24	#3126	Rose Pink Lt.
	#437	#362	#5942	Toast Lt.	T	#813	#161	#7161	Sky Blue Med.
	#469	#267	#6261	Avocado Green Med.		#818	#23	#3281	Antique Rose Very Lt.
O	#471	#266	#6266	Avocado Green Very Lt.	△	#822	#390	#5933	Beige Grey Very Lt.
	#472	#253	#6253	Avocado Green Pale		#826	#161	#7180	Blue Med.
	#644	#830	#5830	Beige Grey Lt.		#827	#160	#7159	Sky Blue Lt.
z	#676	#891	#2305	Honey	■	#899	#52	#3282	Rose Pink Med.
	#677	#886	#5372	Honey Lt.	/	#3799	#236	#8999	Charcoal Dk.
	#700	#228	#6227	Kelly Green		White	#2	#1001	White
V	#702	#226	#6239	Kelly Green Lt.					

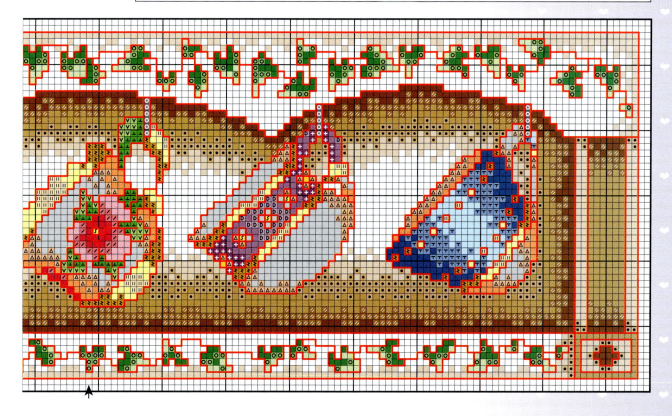

Elegant Magical Touches

Enchanting Delights

Chapter Two

Seasonal Birds

Designed by Mike Vickery

Materials

- 14" x 19" piece of antique white 28-count Monaco

Stitch Count:
110 wide x 184 high

Approximate Design Size:
11-count 10" x 16¾"
14-count 7⅞" x 13¼"
16-count 6⅞" x 11½"
18-count 6⅛" x 10¼"
22-count 5" x 8⅜"
28-count over two
  threads 7⅞" x 13¼"

Instructions

Center and stitch design, stitching over two threads and using two strands floss for Cross-Stitch and one strand floss for Backstitch.

Live with me, and be my love,
And we will all the pleasures prove
That hills and valleys, dales and fields,
And all the craggy mountains yields.

There will we sit upon the rocks,
And see the shepherds feed their flocks,
By shallow rivers, by whose falls
Melodious birds sing madrigals…

From "The Passionate Pilgrim"
by William Shakespeare

Materials

- 12" x 12" piece of white 14-count Aida
- 1 yd. fabric
- 1 yd. contrasting fabric
- 1 yd. ¼" twisted cord

Instructions

1: Select desired numbers from Numbers graph, center and stitch design, using two strands floss for Cross-Stitch and one strand floss for Backstitch and French Knot.

Notes: Trim design to 8" wide x 8¼" tall. From fabric, cut two 4" x 8¼" for A pieces, one 4" x 14" for B piece, one 8¾" x 14" for C piece, one 14" x 19" piece for back and one 10"-diameter circle for bottom. From contrasting fabric, cut two 14" x 19" pieces for front and back lining and one 10"-diameter circle for bottom lining. Use ½" seam allowance.

2: For front, with right sides facing, sew design, A, B and C pieces together according to Front Assembly Diagram.

3: With right sides facing, sew front and back together at sides. With right sides together and easing to fit, sew bottom to bottom opening of front and back pieces, forming tote. Repeat with lining pieces, leaving an opening for turning on one side.

4: With right sides facing, sew tote and lining together around top edge. Turn tote right sides out; slip stitch opening closed. Press top edge.

5: To make casing, sew around the tote 3" below the top edge and again 1" below the first row of stitching. Open the outer seam on each side between the rows of stitching. Insert cord through openings and run it through the casing for drawstring. Knot ends of drawstring as shown in photo.

Stitch Count:
81 wide x 87 high

Approximate Design Size:
11-count 7⅜" x 8"
14-count 5⅞" x 6¼"
16-count 5⅛" x 5½"
18-count 4½" x 4⅞"
22-count 3¾" x 4"

Numbers

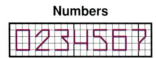

Front Assembly Diagram

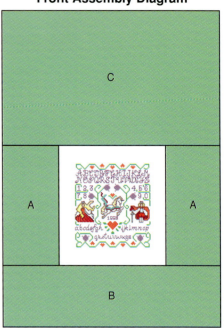

X	B'st	1/4x	Fr	MADIERA DECORA	DMC	ANCHOR	J.&P. COATS	COLORS
			●	#1400	#310	#403	#8403	Black
				#1401	White	#2	#1001	White
				#1410	#762	#234	#8510	Silver Very Lt.
			●	#1433	#550	#102	#4107	Darkest Amethyst
				#1435	#814	#45	#3044	Garnet Very Dk.
				#1439	#304	#1006	#3410	Scarlet
				#1449	#700	#228	#6227	Kelly Green
				#1470	#729	#890	#2875	Old Gold
				#1480	#208	#110	#4301	Lavender Dk.
				#1501	#992	#187	#6186	Aquamarine
				#1513	#948	#1011	#2331	Peach Flesh Very Lt.
				#1521	#209	#109	#4302	Lavender Med.
				#1525	#725	#305	#2294	Topaz Med.
				#1547	#321	#9046	#3500	Cherry Red
				#1553	#775	#128	#7031	Baby Blue

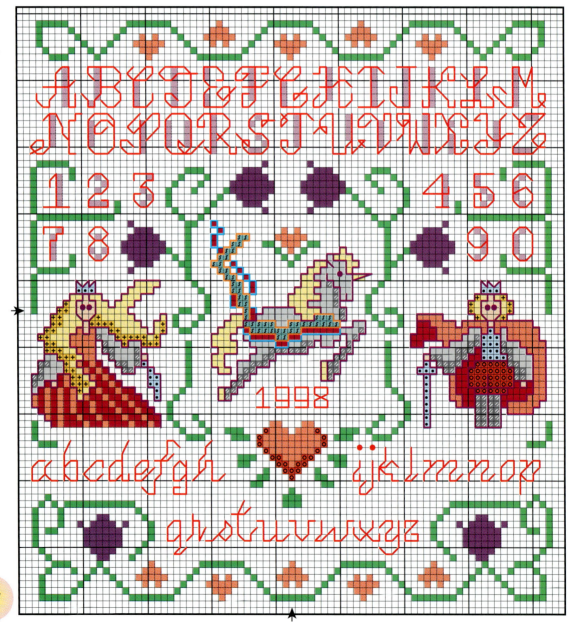

Old Fashioned Flower Basket
PHOTO ON PAGE 35

Materials

- 14" x 25" piece of antique ivory 28-count Cashel Linen®
- ⅓ yd. fabric

Stitch Count:
111 wide x 265 high

Approximate Design Size:
11-count 10⅛" x 24⅛"
14-count 8" x 19"
16-count 7" x 16⅝"
18-count 6¼" x 14¾"
22-count 5⅛" x 12⅛"
28-count over two threads 8" x 19"

Instructions

1: Center and stitch top half of design, continuing bottom half of design by repeating in reverse order, stitching over two threads and using two strands floss for Cross-Stitch and one strand floss for Backstitch.

Notes: Trim 1" from design edges. From fabric, cut one same as design for back. Use ½" seam allowance.

2: With right sides facing, sew design and back together, leaving an opening. Turn right sides out; slip stitch opening closed.

X	B'st	DMC	ANCHOR	J.&P. COATS	COLORS
		#210	#108	#4303	Lavender Lt.
		#333	#119	#4301	Blue Violet Very Dk.
		#433	#358	#5471	Coffee Brown
		#435	#1046	#5371	Toast Dk.
		#436	#1045		Toast
		#471	#266	#5943	Avocado Green Very Lt.
		#501	#878	#6266	Sage Green Dk.
		#503	#876	#6878	Sage Green Lt.
		#552	#99	#6879	Violet Dk.
		#554	#96	#4092	Violet Lt.
		#732	#281	#4104	Khaki Green Med.
		#734	#279	#6010	Khaki Green Lt.
		#742	#303	#6253	Tangerine
		#745	#300	#2302	Topaz Very Lt.
		#746	#275	#2296	Honey Pale
		#792	#941	#2275	Cornflower Blue Dk.
		#793	#176	#7150	Cornflower Blue Lt.
		#906	#256	#7110	Parrot Green Med. Dk.
		#936	#269	#6256	Black Avocado Med.
		#962	#75	#6269	Antique Rose Med.
		#963	#73	#3153	Baby Pink
		#3371	#382	#3173	Darkest Brown
		#3716	#25	#5382	Antique Rose
		#3813	#213	#3125	Sage Green Very Lt.

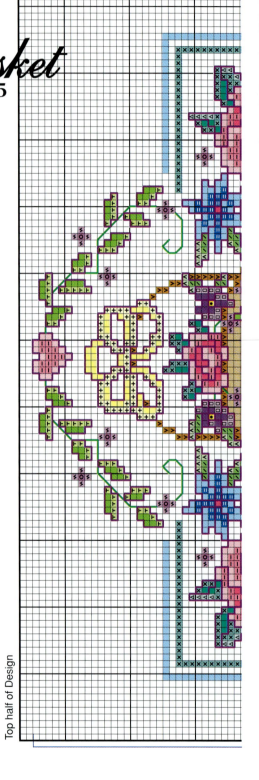

Top half of Design

Repeated design

Materials

- 9" x 13" piece of white 28-count Jobelan®

Instructions

Center and stitch design, stitching over two threads and using two strands floss for Cross-Stitch and one strand floss for Backstitch.

Stitch Count:
45 wide x 92 high

Approximate Design Size:
11-count 4⅛" x 8⅜"
14-count 3¼" x 6⅝"
16-count 2⅞" x 5¾"
18-count 2½" x 5⅛"
22-count 2⅛" x 4¼"
28-count over two
  threads 3¼" x 6⅝"

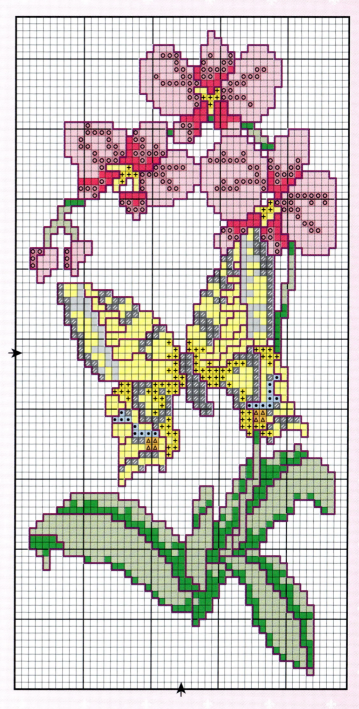

X	B'st	DMC	ANCHOR	J.&P. COATS	COLORS
▨	▧	#310	#403	#8403	Black
▨		#318	#399	#8511	Silver Med.
▨		#319	#218	#6246	Spruce
▨		#320	#215	#6017	Pistachio Green Med.
▨		#335	#38	#3283	Rose Pink Dk.
△		#721	#324	#2324	Orange Spice Med.
+		#725	#305	#2294	Topaz Med.
▨		#727	#293	#2289	Topaz Lt.
▨		#818	#23	#3281	Antique Rose Very Lt.
•		#3325	#129	#7976	Delft Blue
O		#3326	#36	#3126	Rose Pink

Circle of Roses

Designed by Kathleen Hurley

Materials

- 16" x 18" piece of white 28-count Monaco
- ½ yd. fabric
- 1½ yds. ½" piping
- 1½ yds. 1½" lace
- 1½ yds. 2" gathered ruffle
- 12" x 12" pillow form

Stitch Count:
163 wide x 141 high

Approximate Design Size:
11-count 14⅞" x 12⅞"
14-count 11¾" x 10⅛"
16-count 10¼" x 8⅞"
18-count 9⅛" x 7⅞"
22-count 7½" x 6½"
28-count over two threads 11¾" x 10⅛"

Instructions

1: Center and stitch design, stitching over two threads and using two strands floss for Cross-Stitch and one strand floss for Backstitch and Straight Stitch.

Notes: Trim design to 13½" x 13½" for front. From fabric, cut two 9" x 13½" pieces for back. Use ½" seam allowance.

2: With right sides facing, sew to front, first piping, lace and then ruffle.

3: Hem one 13½" edge of each back piece. Place one hemmed edge over the other, overlapping enough to create a 13½" x 13½" back with opening. Baste outside edges together; press.

4: With right sides facing, sew front and back together. Trim seam and turn right sides out; press. Insert pillow form.

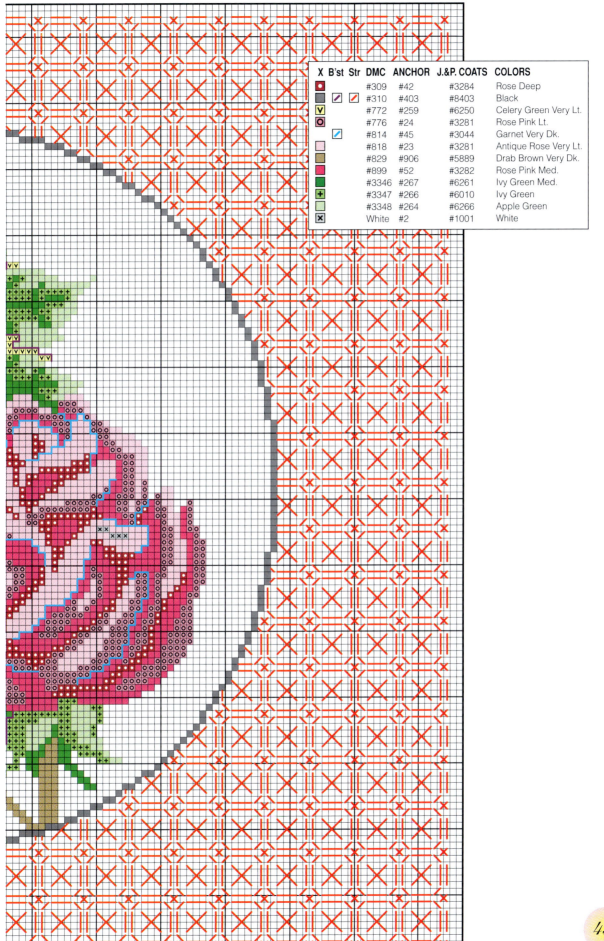

Marriage Sampler

Designed by Brenda Davis

Stitch Count:
100 wide x 161 high

Approximate Design Size:
11-count 9⅛" x 14⅝"
14-count 7¼" x 11½"
16-count 6¼" x 10⅛"
18-count 5⅝" x 9"
22-count 4⅝" x 7⅜"

Materials

- 13" x 18" piece of antique white 14-count Aida

Instructions

Select desired letters and numbers from Alphabet & Numbers graph, center and stitch design, using one strand metallic thread, one strand fine braid or two strands blending filament for Cross-Stitch. Use one strand floss, one strand metallic thread or one strand fine braid for Backstitch and French Knot. Use two strands blending filament for Lazy Daisy Stitch.

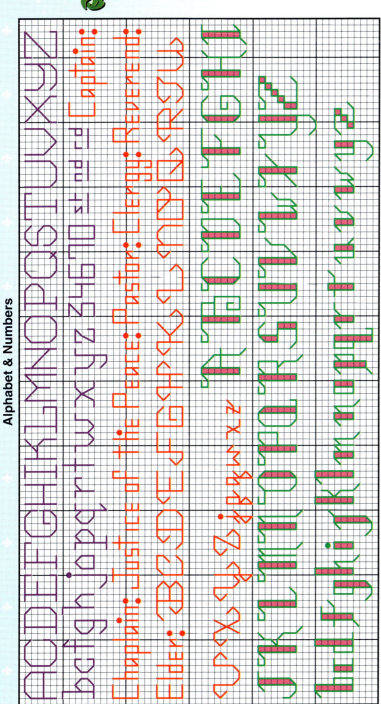

Alphabet & Numbers

X	B'st	¼x	Fr	LzD	DMC	ANCHOR	J.&P. COATS	KREINIK	COLORS
					#310	#403	#8403		Black
						#282z			Lt. Gold (Metallic Thread)
						#284z			Gold (Metallic Thread)
								#095	Starburst (Blending Filament)
								#002HL	Gold (#8 Fine Braid)

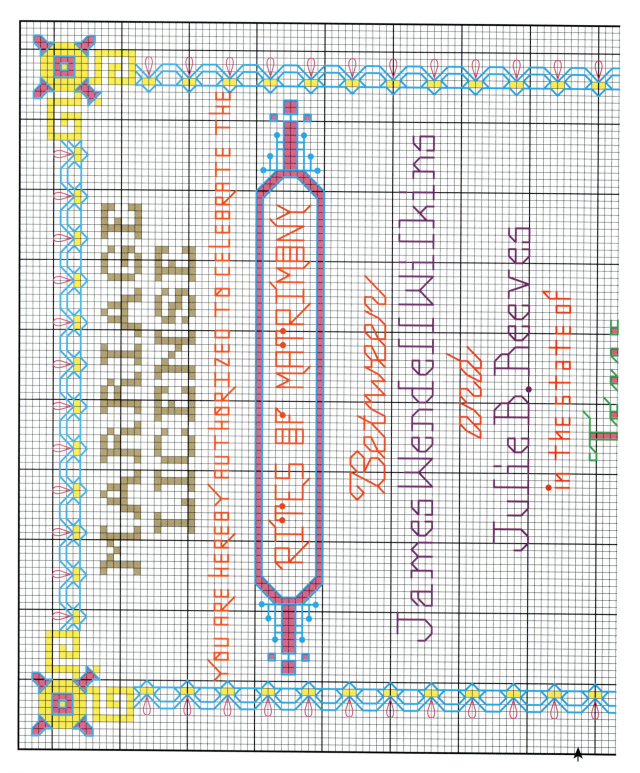

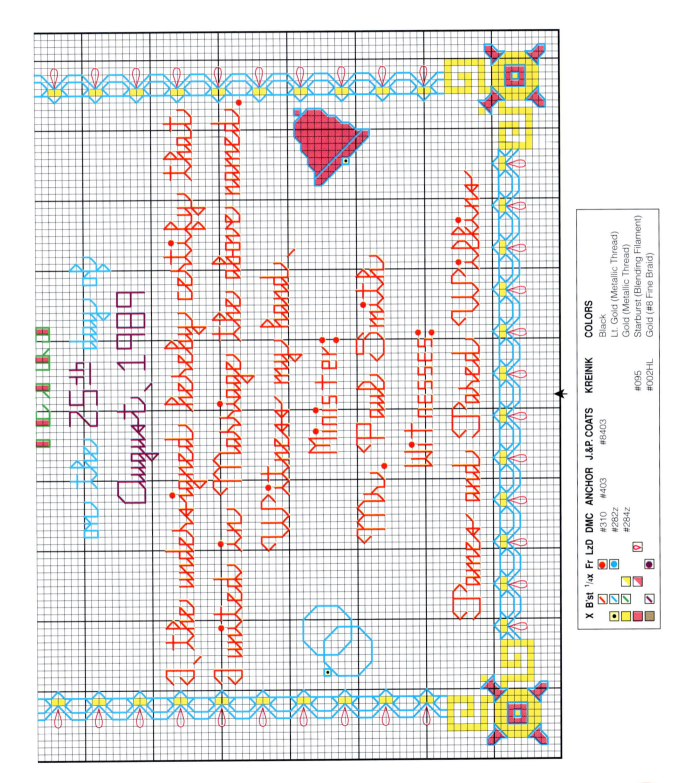

Enchanted Castle

Designed by Mike Vickery

Materials

- 13" x 15" piece of ivory 28-count Monaco

Instructions

Center and stitch design, stitching over two threads and using two strands floss for Cross-Stitch and one strand floss for Backstitch.

Stitch Count:
98 wide x 126 high

Approximate Design Size:
11-count 9" x 11½"
14-count 7" x 9"
16-count 6⅛" x 7⅞"
18-count 5½" x 7"
22-count 4½" x 5¾"
28-count over two threads 7" x 9"

*The splendor falls on castle walls
And snowy summits old in story;
The long light shakes across the lakes,
And the wild cataract leaps in glory. ...
O, hark, O, hear! how thin and clear,
And thinner, clearer, farther going!
O, sweet and far from cliff and scar
The horns of Elfland faintly blowing! ...*

*From "The Splendor Falls"
by Lord Alfred Tennyson*

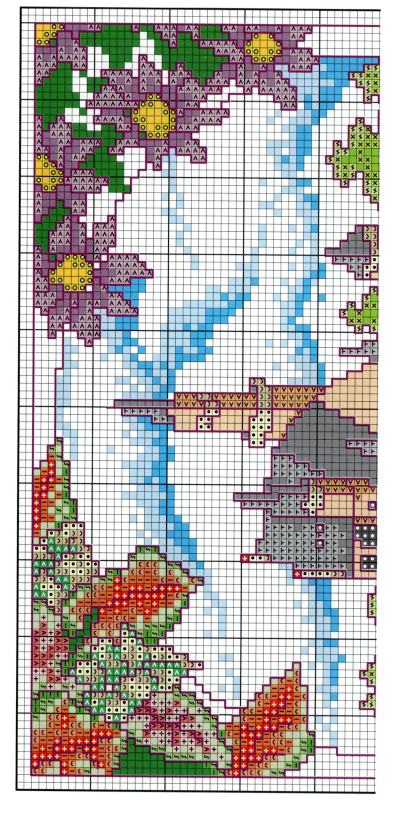

X	DMC	ANCHOR	J.&P. COATS	COLORS
	#208	#110	#4301	Lavender Dk.
	#210	#108	#4303	Lavender Lt.
	#310	#403	#8403	Black
	#434	#310	#5000	Darkest Toast
	#436	#1045	#5943	Toast
	#601	#57	#3128	Cranberry Dk.
	#603	#62	#3153	Cranberry
	#605	#50	#3151	Cranberry Very Lt.
	#646	#8581	#8500	Beaver Grey Dk.
	#666	#46	#3046	Geranium Dk.
	#700	#228	#6227	Kelly Green
	#702	#226	#6239	Kelly Green Lt.

X	DMC	ANCHOR	J.&P. COATS	COLORS
	#704	#256	#6238	Parrot Green Med.
	#725	#305	#2294	Topaz Med.
	#727	#293	#2289	Topaz Lt.
	#775	#128	#7031	Baby Blue
	#776	#24	#3281	Rose Pink Lt.
	#783	#307	#5307	Topaz Very Dk.
	#822	#390	#5933	Beige Grey Very Lt.
	#844	#1041	#8501	Beaver Grey Ultra Dk.
	#890	#218	#6021	Spruce Dk.
	#899	#52	#3282	Rose Pink Med.
	#904	#258	#6258	Darkest Parrot Green
	#905	#257	#6256	Parrot Green Dk.

X	B'st	DMC	ANCHOR	J.&P. COATS	COLORS
		#907	#255	#6001	Parrot Green Lt.
		#910	#229	#6031	Darkest Seafoam Green
		#913	#204	#6225	Seafoam
		#926	#850	#6007	Sea Mist Med.
		#928	#274	#6005	Sea Mist Very Lt.
		#955	#206	#6020	Seafoam Green Very Lt.
		#3705	#35	#3012	Carnation Dk.
		#3706	#33	#3152	Carnation Med.
		#3755	#140	#7976	Delft Blue Med.
		#3799	#236	#8999	Charcoal Dk.
		White	#2	#1001	White

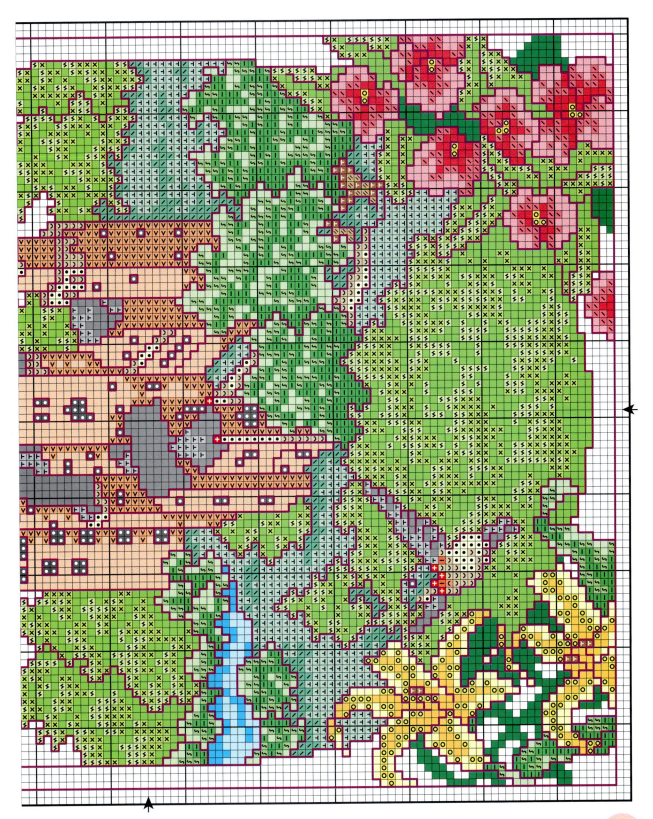

Wonders of Friendship

Enchanting Delights

Chapter Three

Sweet Friendships
Designed by Jacquelyn Fox

Materials

- 10" x 15" piece of beige 14-count Lincoln
- Wooden tray with 5¾" x 9¾" design opening

Instructions

Center and stitch design, using two strands floss for Cross-Stitch and Backstitch and French Knot of "Make Life." Use one strand floss for remaining Backstitch. Position and secure design in tray following manufacturer's instructions.

Stitch Count:
123 wide x 53 high

Approximate Design Size:
11-count 11¼" x 4⅞"
14-count 8⅞" x 3⅞"
16-count 7¾" x 3⅜"
18-count 6⅞" x 3"
22-count 5⅝" x 2½"

Fr	¼x	B'st	X	DMC	ANCHOR	J.&P. COATS	COLORS
				#310	#403	#8403	Black
				#420	#374	#5374	Hazel Nut Dk.
				#676	#891	#2305	Honey
				#680	#901	#2876	Old Gold Dk.
				#743	#302	#2294	Tangerine Lt.
				#792	#941	#7150	Cornflower Blue Dk.
				#794	#175	#7977	Cornflower Blue Very Lt.
				#869	#944	#5374	Warm Brown Med.
				#3345	#268	#6258	Ivy Green Dk.
●				#3348	#264	#6266	Apple Green
				#3371	#382	#5382	Darkest Brown
				#3685	#1028	#3089	Darkest Mauve
				#3688	#66	#3087	Mauve
				#3689	#49	#3086	Mauve Very Lt.
				#3781	#1050	#8500	Coffee Brown
				White	#2	#1001	White

To Have Friends

Designed by Mike Vickery

Materials

- 16" x 18" piece of dirty aida 14-count Aida

Instructions

Center and stitch design, using two strands floss for Cross-Stitch and one strand floss for Backstitch.

Stitch Count:
132 wide x 172 high

Approximate Design Size:
11-count 12" x 15⅝"
14-count 9½" x 12⅜"
16-count 8¼" x 10¾"
18-count 7⅜" x 9⅝"
22-count 6" x 7⅞"

X	B'st	DMC	ANCHOR	J.&P. COATS	COLORS
		#208	#110	#4301	Lavender Dk.
V		#210	#108	#4104	Lavender Lt.
		#211	#342	#4303	Lavender Pale
O		#319	#218	#6246	Spruce
+		#350	#11	#3111	Coral Med.
		#352	#9	#3008	Peach Flesh Dk.
≥		#471	#266	#6266	Avocado Green Very Lt.
—		#472	#253	#6253	Avocado Green Pale
		#644	#830	#5830	Beige Grey Lt.
		#700	#228	#6227	Kelly Green
T		#702	#226	#6239	Kelly Green Lt.
		#704	#256	#6238	Parrot Green Med.
⌣		#725	#305	#2284	Topaz Med.
		#727	#293	#2289	Topaz Lt.
∩		#776	#24	#3281	Rose Pink Lt.
		#791	#178	#7024	Darkest Cornflower Blue
		#794	#175	#7977	Cornflower Blue Very Lt.
		#817	#13	#2335	Nasturtium
X		#822	#390	#5933	Beige Grey Very Lt.
∕		#899	#52	#3282	Rose Pink Med.
>		#910	#229	#6031	Darkest Seafoam Green
		#912	#209	#6266	Seafoam Green Dk.
●		#954	#203	#3030	Seafoam Green Lt.
	∕	#3799	#236	#8999	Charcoal Dk.
≡		#3807	#118	#7110	Cornflower Blue
		White	#2	#1001	White

Fishing Buddies

Designed by Jacquelyn Fox

Materials

- Golf hat with white 14-count Aida insert
- 11" x 13" piece of 14-count waste canvas
- Denim shirt
- Interfacing

Instructions

1: For Hat, center and stitch "Hat" design ¾" from bottom edge of insert, using two strands floss for Cross-Stitch and one strand floss for Backstitch.

2: For Shirt, position and baste interfacing to wrong side of shirt back; next apply waste canvas to back of shirt following manufacturer's instructions. Center and stitch "Shirt" design, using two strands floss for Cross-Stitch and one strand floss for Backstitch.

3: Remove waste canvas from shirt after stitching following manufacturer's instructions. Trim interfacing close to stitching.

Hat
Stitch Count:
51 wide x 30 high

Approximate Design Size:
11-count 4⅝" x 2¾"
14-count 3¾" x 2¼"
16-count 3¼" x 1⅞"
18-count 2⅞" x 1¾"
22-count 2⅜" x 1⅜"

Shirt
Stitch Count:
91 wide x 69 high

Approximate Design Size:
11-count 8⅜" x 6⅜"
14-count 6½" x 5"
16-count 5¾" x 4⅜"
18-count 5⅛" x 3⅞"
22-count 4⅛" x 3⅛"

Hat

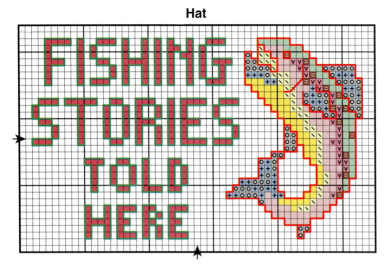

X	B'st	1/4x	DMC	ANCHOR	J.&P. COATS	COLORS
■	/		#221	#897	#3243	Darkest Victorian Rose
V			#224	#893	#3239	Victorian Rose Lt.
		/	#225	#1026	#3066	Victorian Rose Pale
	/		#310	#403	#8403	Black
≥			#321	#9046	#3500	Cherry Red
≡			#435	#1046	#5371	Toast Dk.
			#522	#860	#6316	Fern Green Med.
			#676	#891	#2305	Honey
\			#746	#275	#2274	Honey Pale
			#924	#851	#6008	Darkest Sea Mist
+			#927	#848	#6006	Sea Mist Lt.
O			#3768	#779	#6007	Sea Mist Dk.
•	/		White	#2	#1001	White

Shirt

Rose Heart

PHOTO ON PAGE 63

Materials

- 12" x 13" piece of evening rose 14-count Yorkshire Aida
- 1 yd. fabric
- 1 yd. ⅛" piping
- 1¾ yds. ¼" piping
- 1¾ yds. 1½" gathered eyelet
- 12" x 16" pillow form

Instructions

Note: If desired, initial and date work, as shown in photo.

1: Center and stitch design, using two strands floss for Cross-Stitch and one strand floss or fine braid for Backstitch and Straight Stitch.

Notes: Trim design to 7½" x 9". From fabric, cut two 4" x 17½" for A pieces, two 5¼" x 7½" for B pieces, two 12" x 13½" pieces for back and three 5" x 42" pieces for ruffle. Use ½" seam allowance.

2: With right sides facing, sew ⅛" piping to design. With right sides facing, sew design, A and B pieces together according to Front Assembly Diagram, forming front.

3: For ruffle, with right sides facing, sew short ends of fabric pieces together, forming ring. Fold wrong sides together; press. Gather unfinished edges to fit around outside edges of front.

4: With right sides facing, sew to front, first ¼" piping, eyelet and then ruffle.

5: Hem one 13½" edge of each back piece. Place one hemmed edge over the other, overlapping enough to create a 13½" x 17½" back with opening. Baste outside edges together; press.

6: With right sides facing, sew front and back together. Trim seam and turn right sides out; press. Insert pillow form.

Stitch Count:
97 wide x 78 high

Approximate Design Size:
11-count 8⅞" x 7⅛"
14-count 7" x 5⅝"
16-count 6⅛" x 4⅞"
18-count 5⅜" x 4⅜"
22-count 4½" x 3⅝"

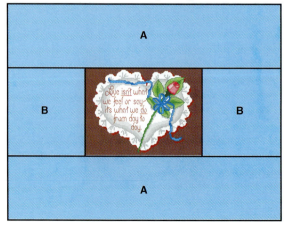

Front Assembly Diagram

X	B'st	1/4x	3/4x	Str	MADEIRA SILK	MADEIRA DECORA	DMC	ANCHOR	J.&P. COATS	KREINIK(#8)	COLORS
					#0502		#818	#23	#3281		Antique Rose Very Lt.
					#0503		#776	#24	#3126		Rose Pink Lt.
					#0504		#3326	#36	#3126		Rose Pink
					#0511		#498	#1005	#3000		Garnet
					#0811		#221	#897	#3243		Darkest Victorian Rose held with
					#0812		#223	#895	#3240		Victorian Rose Med.
					#0812		#223	#895	#3240		Victorian Rose Med.
					#1312		#367	#217	#6018		Pistachio Green Dk.
					#1407		#3346	#267	#6261		Ivy Green Med.
					#1408		#3347	#266	#6010		Ivy Green
					#1603		#3364	#260	#6266		Celery Green Lt.
					#1709		#928	#274	#6005		Sea Mist Very Lt.
					#1803		#415	#398	#8398		Silver held with
					#1804		#762	#234	#8510		Silver Very Lt.
					#1804		#762	#234	#8510		Silver Very Lt.
					#1804		#762	#234	#8510		Silver Very Lt. held with
					White		White	#2	#1001		White
					White		White	#2	#1001		White
						#1475	#3761	#928	#7053		Sky Blue Very Lt.
						#1495	#996	#433	#7001		Electric Blue
						#1496	#995	#410	#7010		Imperial Blue
										#001	Silver

Materials

- 11" x 11" piece of light blue 16-count Aida

Instructions

Center and stitch design, using two strands floss for Cross-Stitch and one strand floss for Backstitch.

Stitch Count:
80 wide x 81 high

Approximate Design Size:
11-count 7 3/8" x 7 3/8"
14-count 5 3/4" x 5 7/8"
16-count 5" x 5 1/8"
18-count 4 1/2" x 4 1/2"
22-count 3 5/8" x 3 3/4"

X	B'st	1/4x	DMC	ANCHOR	J.&P. COATS	COLORS
T			#211	#342	#4303	Lavender Pale
V			#300	#352	#5349	Mahogany Very Dk.
•	/		#310	#403	#8403	Black
	/		#318	#399	#8511	Silver Med.
			#341	#117	#7005	Blue Violet Lt.
	/		#550	#102	#4107	Darkest Amethyst
	/		#553	#98	#4097	Violet Med.
	/		#676	#891	#2305	Honey
	/		#921	#1003	#2338	Copper
O			#930	#1035	#7052	Blue Denim Dk.
			#3371	#382	#5382	Darkest Brown
	/		#3750	#1036	#7980	Darkest Blue Denim
			#3770	#1009	#3334	Cream Lt.
+			#3827	#311	#5351	Golden Brown Lt.
			White	#2	#1001	White

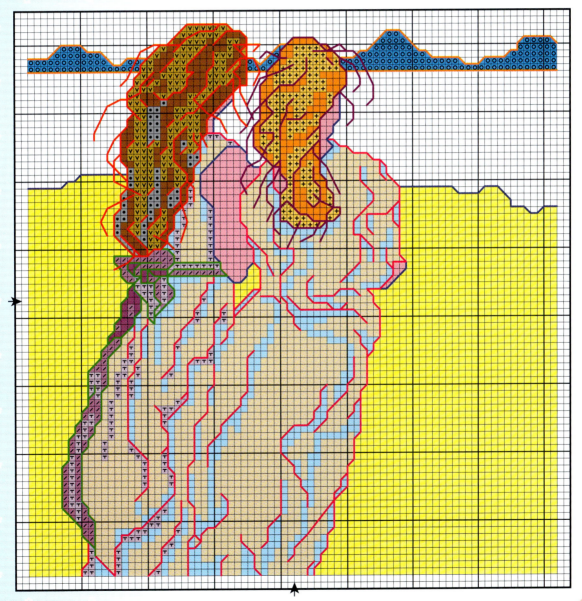

67

Materials

- 11" x 11" piece of light blue 14-count Aida

Stitch Count:
75 wide x 69 high

Approximate Design Size:
11-count 6⅞" x 6⅜"
14-count 5⅜" x 5"
16-count 4¾" x 4⅜"
18-count 4¼" x 3⅞"
22-count 3½" x 3⅛"

Instructions

Center and stitch design, using two strands floss for Cross-Stitch and one strand floss for Backstitch and French Knot.

X	B'st	¼x	Fr	DMC	ANCHOR	J.&P. COATS	COLORS
				#309	#42	#3284	Rose Deep
				#310	#403	#8403	Black
				#561	#212	#6211	Jade Very Dk.
				#606	#334	#2334	Bright Orange Red
				#743	#302	#2294	Tangerine Lt.
				#910	#229	#6031	Darkest Seafoam Green
				#955	#206	#6020	Seafoam Green Very Lt.
				#961	#76	#3176	Antique Rose Dk.
				White	#2	#1001	White

A true friend overlooks your broken down gate and admires the flowers in your garden.

A Mother's Love
Designed by Ursula Michael

Materials

- 13¾" piece of 5½"-wide ivory 14-count Stitchband
- 7" wooden bell pull
- ⅓ yd. ribbon

Instructions

1: Center and stitch design, using two strands floss for Cross-Stitch and one strand floss for Backstitch.

2: Fold under a ¾" hem on short ends of design; slip stitch in place.

3: Insert bell pull into folded ends as shown in photo, following manufacturer's instructions. Tie ribbon to each end of bell pull for hanger as shown.

Stitch Count:
46 wide x 136 high

Approximate Design Size:
11-count 4¼" x 12⅜"
14-count 3⅜" x 9¾"
16-count 2⅞" x 8½"
18-count 2⅝" x 7⅝"
22-count 2⅛" x 6¼"

X	B'st	¼x	DMC	ANCHOR	J.&P. COATS	COLORS
■		◢	#319	#218	#6246	Spruce
	◢		#498	#1005	#3000	Garnet
■		◢	#726	#295	#2295	Topaz
	◢		#796	#133	#7100	Royal Blue
■		◢	#798	#131	#7022	Blueberry Dk.
■		◢	#800	#144	#7020	Blueberry Pale
V		◢	#809	#130	#7021	Blueberry Lt.
■		◢	#961	#76	#3176	Antique Rose Dk.
O	◢		#3347	#266	#6010	Ivy Green
■			#3348	#264	#6266	Apple Green
■		◢	#3716	#25	#3125	Antique Rose

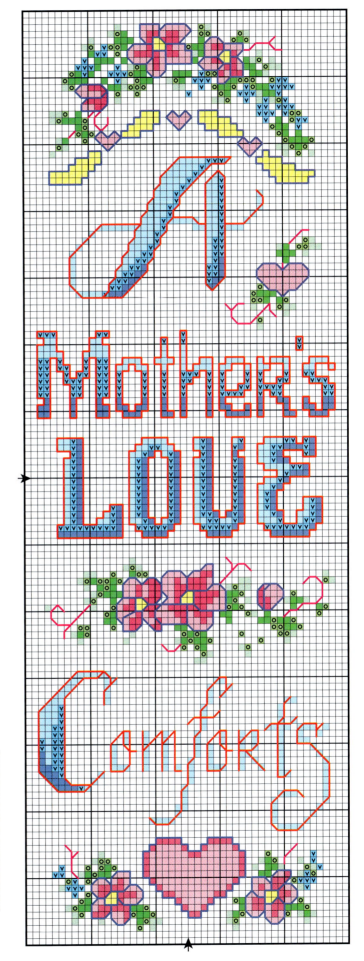

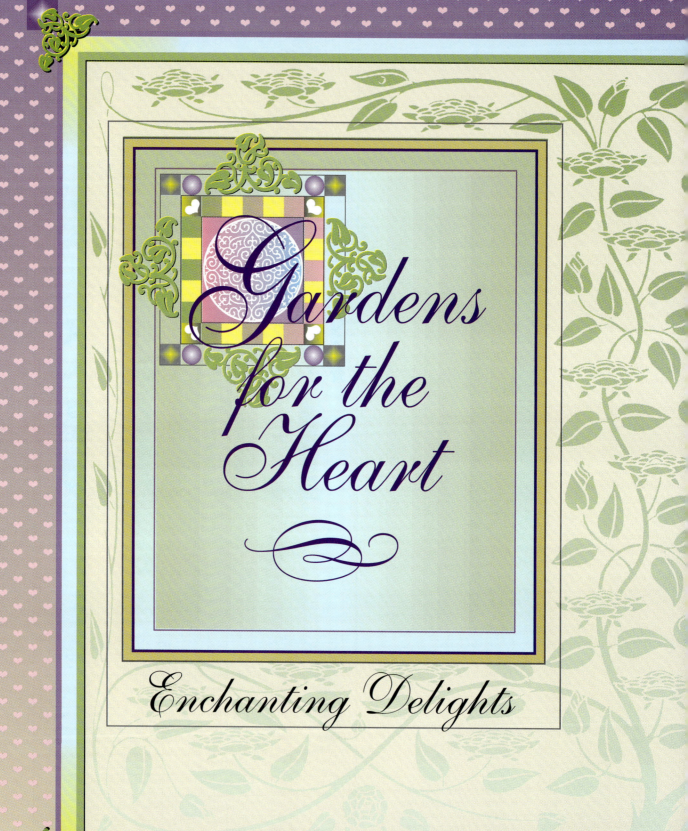

Chapter Four

Beauty Blooms

Designed by Jacquelyn Fox

Materials

- 11" x 11" piece of carnation 28-count Pastel Linen
- Basket of choice
- Batting
- Lightweight cardboard
- ¾ yd. lace
- Craft glue or glue gun

Stitch Count:
73 wide x 74 high

Approximate Design Size:
11-count 6⅝" x 6¾"
14-count 5¼" x 5⅜"
16-count 4⅝" x 4⅝"
18-count 4⅛" x 4⅛"
22-count 3⅜" x 3⅜"
28-count over two
 threads 5¼" x 5⅜"

Instructions

1: Center and stitch design, stitching over two threads and using two strands floss for Cross-Stitch and Backstitch of lettering and vines. Use two strands floss for French Knot and Lazy Daisy Stitch and one strand floss for remaining Backstitch.

Note: From batting and cardboard, cut one each 6¼" x 6¼".

2: Center and mount design over batting and cardboard. Glue lace around back outside edges of mounted design.

3: Position and glue mounted design to basket as shown in photo.

Dewdrops fill my garden,
The kiss of God's great love.
Blossoms in delicate arrangement,
Placed by heaven from above.
The Master's hand again embraced,
The beauty of this garden fair,
The touch of God on display, …

From "The Beauty of the Heart"
by Jannie Birch

X	B'st	1/4x	Fr	LzD	DMC	ANCHOR	J.&P. COATS	COLORS
	/				#208	#110	#4301	Lavender Dk.
V	/				#210	#108	#4303	Lavender Lt.
O	/				#741	#304	#2314	Tangerine Dk.
					#744	#301	#2293	Tangerine Pale
	/		●		#791	#178	#7024	Darkest Cornflower Blue
	/				#793	#176	#7110	Cornflower Blue Lt.
					#963	#73	#3173	Baby Pink
	/				#3731	#76	#3176	Dusty Rose
		/			#3733	#75	#3126	Dusty Rose Lt.
	/			V	#3815	#216	#6876	Celdon Green Dk.

Indigo

PHOTO ON PAGE 77

The Break of Dawn

Morning has broken,
The bird on the wing,
The heavens are singing,
A love song to me.
Azure as the sky,
Indigo shaded of blue,
Your song so exquisite,
So harmonious and true.
Please stay awhile and sing for me,
Natures song of love,
Only a bluebird can sing.

By Jannie Birch

Materials

- 11" x 16" piece of cream 28-count Meran

Instructions

Center and stitch design, stitching over two threads and using two strands floss for Cross-Stitch and Straight Stitch. Use one strand floss for Backstitch and French Knot.

Stitch Count:
138 wide x 74 high

Approximate Design Size:
11-count 12⅝" x 6¾"
14-count 9⅞" x 5⅜"
16-count 8⅝" x 4⅝"
18-count 7¾" x 4⅛"
22-count 6⅜" x 3⅜"
28-count over two threads 9⅞" x 5⅜"

DMC	ANCHOR	J.&P. COATS	COLORS
#317	#400	#8512	Darkest Silver
#318	#399	#8511	Silver Med.
#347	#1025	#3013	Rose Coral Dk.
#413	#401	#8514	Charcoal
#415	#398	#8398	Silver
#469	#267	#6261	Avocado Green Med.
#470	#266	#6010	Avocado Green Lt.
#471	#265	#6266	Avocado Green Very Lt.
#744	#301	#2293	Tangerine Pale
#745	#300	#2296	Topaz Very Lt.
#746	#275	#2275	Honey Pale
#760	#1022	#3071	Salmon
#761	#1021	#3069	Salmon Lt.
#797	#132	#7143	Deep Blueberry
#798	#131	#7022	Blueberry Dk. held with
#799	#136	#7030	Blueberry Med.
#798	#131	#7022	Blueberry Dk. held with
#995	#410	#7010	Imperial Blue
#839	#380	#5478	Darkest Pecan
#838	#360	#5360	Pecan Dk.
#840	#379	#5379	Pecan Med.
#936	#269	#6269	Black Avocado Med.
#937	#268	#6268	Black Avocado
#948	#1011	#2331	Peach Flesh Very Lt.
#995	#410	#7010	Imperial Blue held with
#996	#433	#7001	Electric Blue
#996	#433	#7001	Electric Blue
#3328	#1024	#3111	Salmon Dk.
#3712	#1023	#3011	Salmon Med.
#3713	#1020	#3068	Salmon Very Lt.
#3770	#1009	#3334	Cream Lt.
#3799	#236	#8999	Charcoal Dk.
#30776 (Rayon)	#24	#3281	Rose Pink Lt.

Perfect Pansies

Designed by Ursula Michael

Materials

- One 7" x 11" piece and one 8" x 9" piece of amber 28-count Linen
- 9" x 11" piece of brown perforated paper
- 12 cm brass bell pull
- Needlework card with 2½" x 3½" oval opening
- Scrap of fabric
- ⅜ yd. 1¼" lace
- ⅝ yd. decorative trim
- Three 2" tassels
- Craft glue or glue gun

Pansy Trio & Beaded Pansies Stitch Count:
38 wide x 28 high

Approximate Design Size:
11-count 3½" x 2⅝"
14-count 2¾" x 2"
16-count 2⅜" x 1¾"
18-count 2⅛" x 1⅝"
22-count 1¾" x 1⅜"
28-count over two threads 2¾" x 2"

Instructions

1: For Sachet, center and stitch "Pansy Trio" design onto 7" x 11" piece of Linen, stitching over two threads and using two strands floss for Cross-Stitch and one strand floss for Backstitch.

Notes: From decorative trim, cut one 12" piece. Use ½" seam allowance.

2: With right sides facing, sew 7" edges of design together. Position seam in center back; press. Sew bottom edges together; turn right sides out. Press under ½" hem on top edge. Sew lace to inside of top edge; sew trim around outside of top edge. Secure one tassel to each bottom corner as shown in photo.

3: For Bell Pull, center and stitch "Pansy Trio" design onto 8" x 9" piece of Linen, stitching over two threads and using two strands floss for Cross-Stitch and one strand for Backstitch.

Notes: Trim design to 5½" x 8½"; trim bottom edge into a "V" shape as shown, forming front. From fabric, cut one same as front for back. Use ½" seam allowance.

4: With right sides facing,

81

sew front and back together, leaving a small opening. Turn right sides out; slip stitch opening closed. Fold under ½" on top edge. Insert folded edge through bell pull; slip stitch folded edge in place. Sew remaining tassel to bottom edge as shown.

5: For Card, center and stitch "Beaded Pansies" design onto perforated paper, using one strand coordinating floss for securing beads.

6: Trim and insert design into card following manufacturer's instructions. Glue remaining trim to card as shown.

Pansy Trio

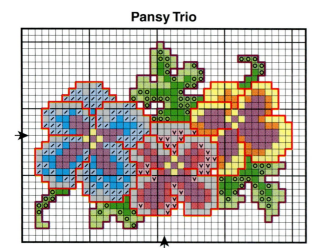

Pansy Trio					
X	B'st	DMC	ANCHOR	J.&P. COATS	COLORS
▨	╱	#208	#110	#4301	Lavender Dk.
▨		#704	#256	#6238	Parrot Green Med.
▨		#726	#295	#2295	Topaz
▨		#742	#303	#2302	Tangerine
▨		#798	#131	#7022	Blueberry Dk.
╱		#800	#144	#7020	Blueberry Pale
▨	╱	#890	#218	#6021	Spruce Dk.
O		#988	#243	#6258	Willow Green Med.
▨		#3688	#66	#3087	Mauve
V		#3689	#49	#3086	Mauve Very Lt.
▨		White	#2	#1001	White

Beaded Pansies

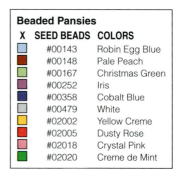

Beaded Pansies		
X	SEED BEADS	COLORS
▨	#00143	Robin Egg Blue
▨	#00148	Pale Peach
▨	#00167	Christmas Green
▨	#00252	Iris
▨	#00358	Cobalt Blue
▨	#00479	White
▨	#02002	Yellow Creme
▨	#02005	Dusty Rose
▨	#02018	Crystal Pink
▨	#02020	Creme de Mint

Spring Bouquets
PHOTO ON PAGE 83

Materials for One

- 10" x 13" piece of white 28-count Lugana®
- ½ yd. fabric
- ¾ yd. ½" trim (Entredeaux trim was used on projects shown)

Instructions

1: Center and stitch design of choice, stitching over two threads and using two strands floss for Cross-Stitch and one strand floss for Backstitch and Lazy Daisy Stitch.

Notes: Trim design to 5" x 12½" for center. From fabric, cut one 5" x 12½" piece for bottom and one 12½" x 13¾" piece for top. Cut trim in half. Use ¼" seam allowance.

2: With right sides facing, sew top, center, bottom and trim pieces together according to Towel Assembly Diagram, forming towel. Hem outside edges of towel, folding corners as you sew.

Towel Assembly Diagram

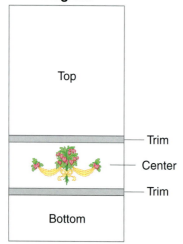

Fuchsia
Stitch Count:
98 wide x 53 high
Approximate Design Size:
11-count 9 x 4⅞"
14-count 7" x 3⅞"
16-count 6⅛" x 3⅜"
18-count 5½" x 3"
22-count 4½" x 2½"
28-count over two threads 7" x 3⅞"

Violet
Stitch Count:
99 wide x 51 high
Approximate Design Size:
11-count 9 x 4⅝"
14-count 7⅛" x 3¾"
16-count 6¼" x 3¼"
18-count 5½" x 2⅞"
22-count 4½" x 2⅜"
28-count over two threads 7⅛" x 3¾"

Fuchsia							
X	B'st	¼x	LzD	DMC	ANCHOR	J.&P. COATS	COLORS
V	/			#367	#217	#6018	Pistachio Green Dk.
				#368	#214	#6016	Pistachio Green Lt.
X				#726	#295	#2295	Topaz
				#746	#275	#2275	Honey Pale
	/			#780	#310	#5000	Russet Dk.
				#783	#307	#5307	Topaz Very Dk.
	/			#890	#218	#6021	Spruce Dk.
O				#962	#75	#3153	Antique Rose Med.
			Q	#963	#73	#3173	Baby Pink
				#3731	#76	#3176	Dusty Rose
	/			#3803	#69	#3089	Mauve Dk.

Violet							
X	B'st	¼x	LzD	DMC	ANCHOR	J.&P. COATS	COLORS
?				#208	#110	#4301	Lavender Dk.
				#210	#108	#4303	Lavender Lt.
		/		#319	#218	#6246	Spruce
	/			#367	#217	#6018	Pistachio Green Dk.
				#368	#214	#6016	Pistachio Green Lt.
	/			#550	#102	#4107	Darkest Amethyst
				#552	#99	#4092	Violet Dk.
				#726	#295	#2295	Topaz
				#890	#218	#6021	Spruce Dk.
•	/			#961	#76	#3176	Antique Rose Dk.
				#963	#73	#3173	Baby Pink
	/			#3350	#59	#3004	Dusty Rose Very Dk.

Fuchsia

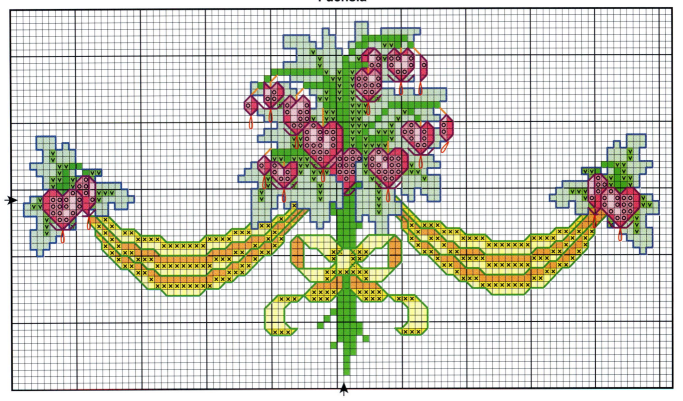

Violet

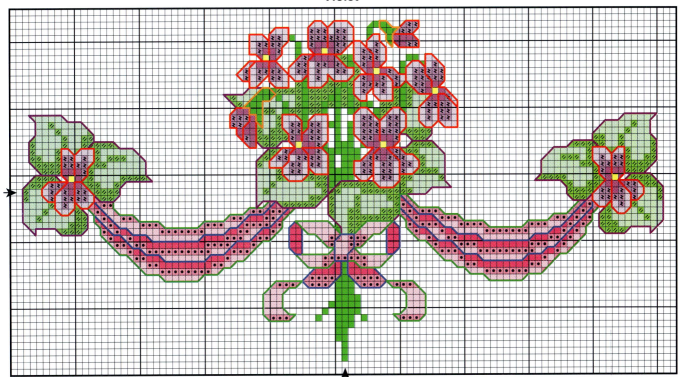

For Wrent
Designed by Dayna Stedry

Stitch Count:
43 wide x 92 high

Approximate Design Size:
11-count 4" x 8⅜"
14-count 3⅛" x 6⅝"
16-count 2¾" x 5¾"
18-count 2⅜" x 5⅛"
22-count 2" x 4¼"

Materials

- 9" x 13" piece of white 14-count Aida
- ⅝ yd. 3 mm bead string
- Scrap of fabric
- 3¾" x 7¼" piece of foam core board
- 22½" piece of ¼" dowel rod
- ¼ yd. ribbon
- Six miniature roses
- Small amount baby's breath
- Craft glue or glue gun

Instructions

1: Center and stitch design, using three strands floss for Cross-Stitch and two strands floss for Backstitch.

Note: Trim design to 4" x 7½".

2: Press design edges under ¼". Tack bead string around front outside edges of design as shown in photo.

3: Cover foam core board with fabric; center and glue design to covered board.

4: Glue covered board to dowel rod as shown. Decorate with ribbon, roses, and baby's breath as shown or as desired.

X	B'st	DMC	ANCHOR	J.&P. COATS	COLORS
		#349	#13	#2335	Coral Dk.
		#352	#9	#3008	Peach Flesh Dk.
		#368	#214	#6016	Pistachio Green Lt.
		#745	#300	#2296	Topaz Very Lt.
		#746	#275	#2275	Honey Pale
		#760	#1022	#3069	Salmon
		#775	#128	#7031	Baby Blue
		#840	#379	#5379	Pecan Med.
		#842	#368	#5933	Pecan Cream
		#931	#1034	#7051	Blue Denim Med.
		#932	#1033	#7050	Blue Denim Lt.
		#948	#1011	#2331	Peach Flesh Very Lt.
		#3713	#1020	#3068	Salmon Very Lt.

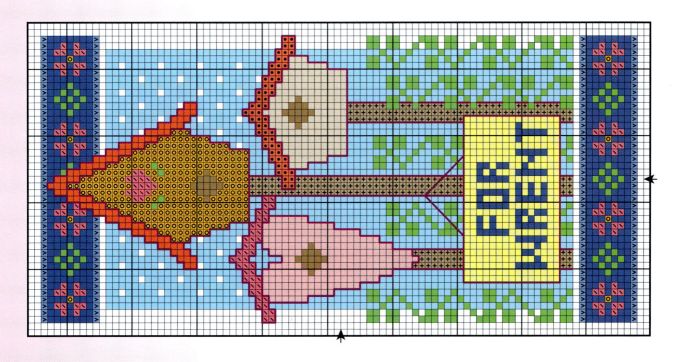

Plant a Garden

Designed by Christine Hendricks

Materials

- 11" x 14" piece of ivory 14-count Aida
- 11" x 17" bulletin board
- 1 yd. ½" bias tape
- 1⅝ yds. 1½" lace
- 3" bow
- Craft glue or glue gun

Stitch Count:
73 wide x 108 high

Approximate Design Size:
11-count 6⅝" x 9⅞"
14-count 5¼" x 7⅞"
16-count 4⅝" x 6¾"
18-count 4⅛" x 6"
22-count 3⅜" x 5"

Instructions

1: Center and stitch design, using two strands floss for Cross-Stitch and one strand floss for Backstitch and French Knot. Use three strands floss for Straight Stitch.

Note: Trim design to 6¾" x 9¼".

2: Press under ½" on design edges. Sew bias tape around back outside edges of design; glue design to bulletin board as shown in photo.

3: Glue lace around edges of bulletin board and bow to bottom of bulletin board as shown.

Though trials may befall me,
Afflictions cast me down,
Through truth and spirit,
I shall rise and find the higher ground.
By faith I'll keep believing,
And trusting in His word.
For in my walk throughout this life,
I've planted His holy verse…

From "The Garden of Life"
By Jannie Birch

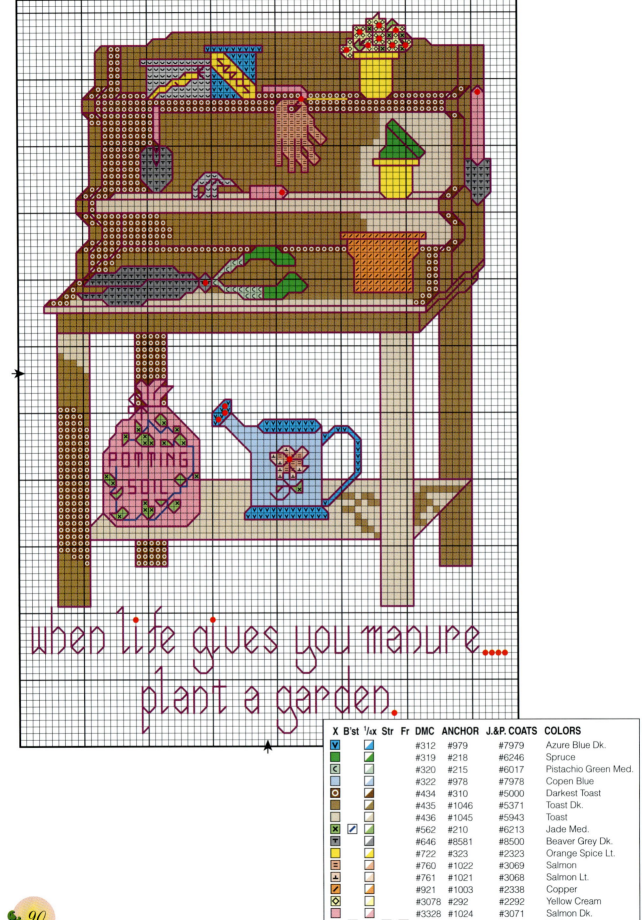

God's Garden

PHOTO ON PAGE 91

Stitch Count:
128 wide x 94 high

Approximate Design Size:
11-count 11⅝" x 8⅝"
14-count 9¼" x 6¾"
16-count 8" x 5⅞"
18-count 7⅛" x 5¼"
22-count 5⅞" x 4⅜"

Materials

- 13" x 15" piece of light blue 14-count Aida

Instructions

Center and stitch design, using two strands floss for Cross-Stitch and one strand floss for Backstitch and French Knot.

DMC	ANCHOR	J.&P. COATS	COLORS
#310	#403	#8403	Black
#353	#8	#3006	Peach Flesh Med.
#368	#214	#6016	Pistachio Green Lt.
#414	#235	#8513	Silver Dk.
#415	#398	#8398	Silver
#434	#310	#5000	Darkest Toast
#606	#334	#2334	Bright Orange Red
#677	#886	#5372	Honey Lt.
#700	#228	#6227	Kelly Green
#702	#226	#6239	Kelly Green Lt.
#704	#256	#6238	Parrot Green Med.
#729	#890	#2875	Old Gold
#740	#316	#2327	Pumpkin Bright
#754	#1012	#2331	Peach Flesh Lt.
#776	#24	#3281	Rose Pink Lt.
#799	#136	#7030	Blueberry Med.
#800	#144	#7020	Blueberry Pale
#801	#359	#5472	Coffee Brown Dk.
#899	#52	#3282	Rose Pink Med.
#972	#298	#2298	Tangerine Med.
#973	#297	#2290	Lemon
White	#2	#1001	White

My Garden of Love

On fertile ground seeds are sown,
When watered the truth of God can grow.
Like flowers in my garden sweet,
The wonder of God becomes complete.
From a single seed can arise,
Awesome beauty held on high.
The rain from heaven nourishes the seed,
As the word of God nurtures me.

By Jannie Birch

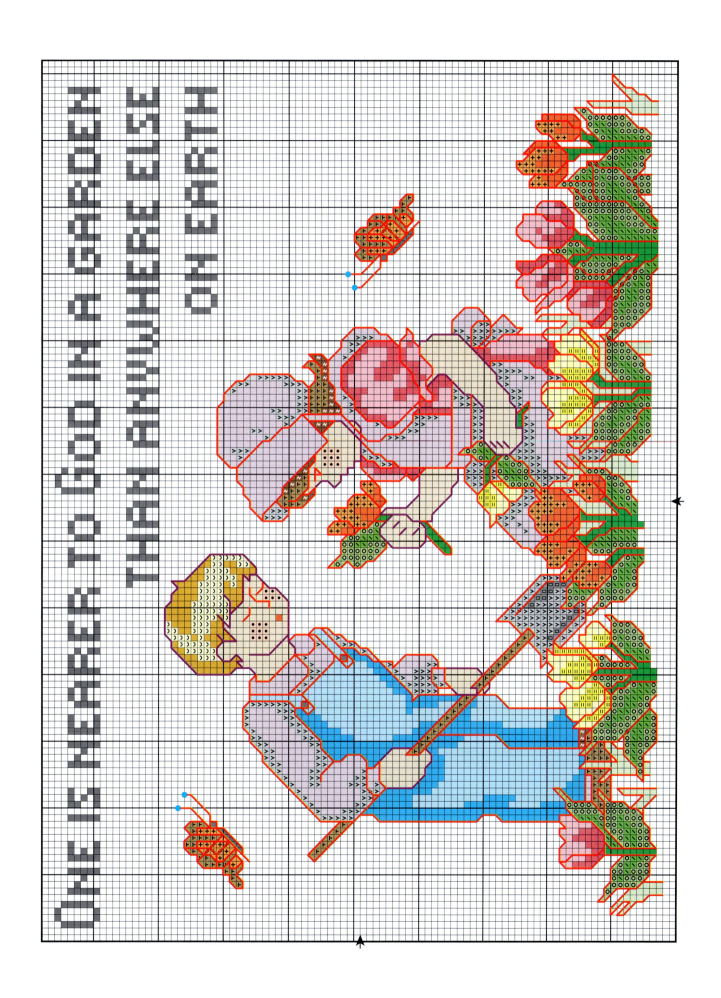

Garden Alphabet
Designed by Dayna Stedry

Materials
- 14" x 16" piece of platinum 14-count Aida

Instructions
Center and stitch design, using three strands floss for Cross-Stitch.

Stitch Count:
95 wide x 135 high

Approximate Design Size:
11-count 8⅝" x 12⅜"
14-count 6⅞" x 9¾"
16-count 6" x 8½"
18-count 5⅜" x 7½"
22-count 4⅜" x 6⅛"

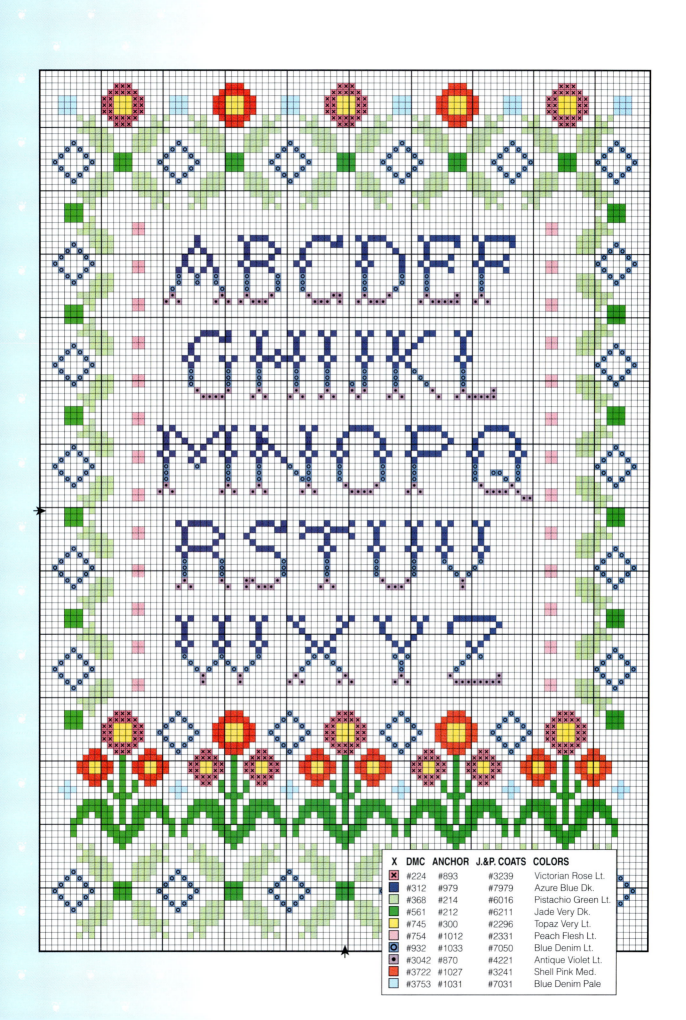

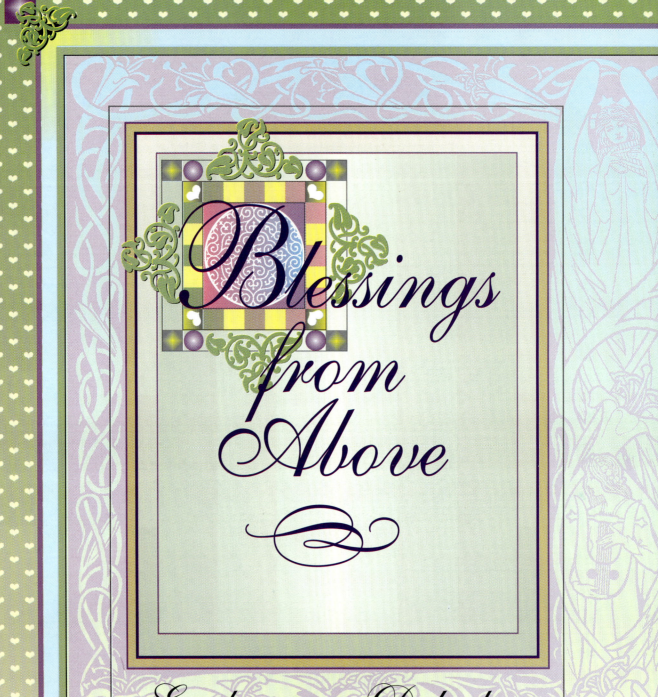

Blessings from Above

Enchanting Delights

Chapter Five

Believing

Designed by Tina Zednick

Materials

- 15" x 16" piece of khaki 28-count evenweave fabric

Stitch Count:
120 wide x 133 high

Approximate Design Size:
11-count 11" x 12⅛"
14-count 8⅝" x 9½"
16-count 7½" x 8⅜"
18-count 6¾" x 7⅜"
22-count 5½" x 6⅛"
28-count over two threads 8⅝" x 9½"

Instructions

Select desired letters and numbers for name and date, center and stitch design, stitching over two threads and using two strands floss for Cross-Stitch, Backstitch, Smyrna Stitch (see illustration) and French Knot. Stitch over four threads and use two strands floss for Four-sided Stitch (see illustration).

Believe on Me

Faith is merely believing,
Leave no room for doubt,
For His word tells us this.
Believe in what the Father says,
For life is what He gives.
We say we must "See to believe,"
We must "Believe first then we will see,"
God will provide our every need,
That's why He is our King.
The day will come when He will call,
His children nigh to Him,
Believe in your heart with all you have,
For the Lord will come again.

By Jannie Birch

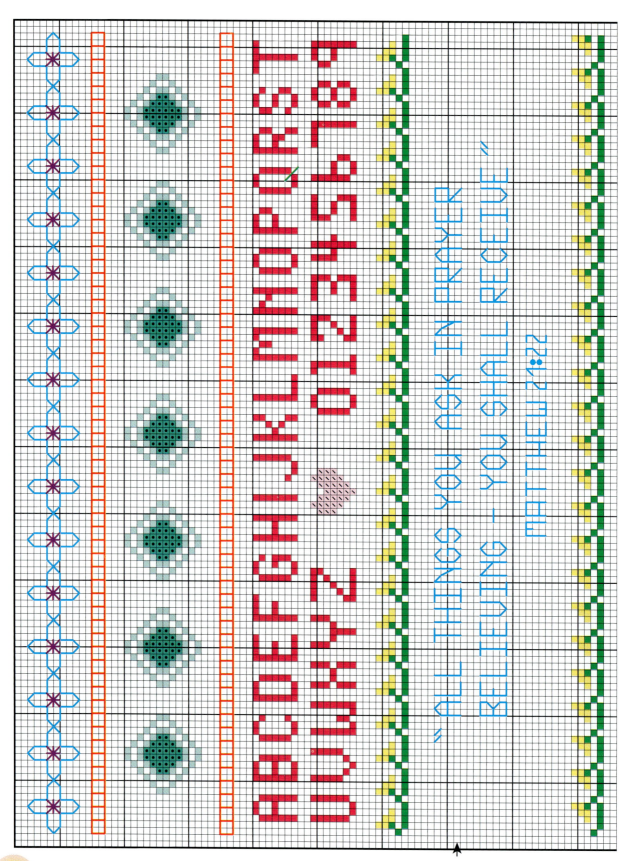

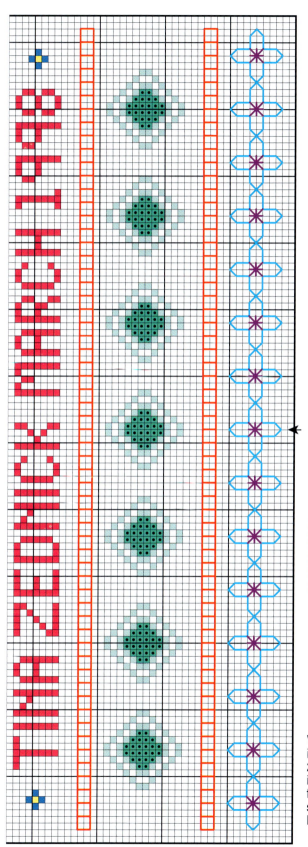

X	B'st	Smy	Fr	FSd	DMC	ANCHOR	J.&P. COATS	COLORS
					#224	#893	#3239	Victorian Rose Lt.
					#312	#979	#7979	Azure Blue Dk.
					#890	#218	#6021	Spruce Dk.
					#943	#188	#6187	Aquamarine Dk.
					#959	#186	#6185	Aquamarine Lt.
					#972	#298	#2298	Tangerine Med.
					#3328	#1024	#3071	Salmon Dk.
					Ecru	#387	#1002	Ecru

Smyrna Stitch

Four-sided Stitch

Work from right to left and stitch over four threads in each direction. **(1)** To start, come up at 1, go in at 2, exit at 3. **(2)** Go in at 1 and come up at 4. **(3)** Go in at 2, exit at 3. **(4)** Go in at 2, exit at 3 (last bar of first Four-sided Stitch forms first bar of second stitch). **(5)** Repeat steps 1-4 until row is completed. Pull each stitch tight.

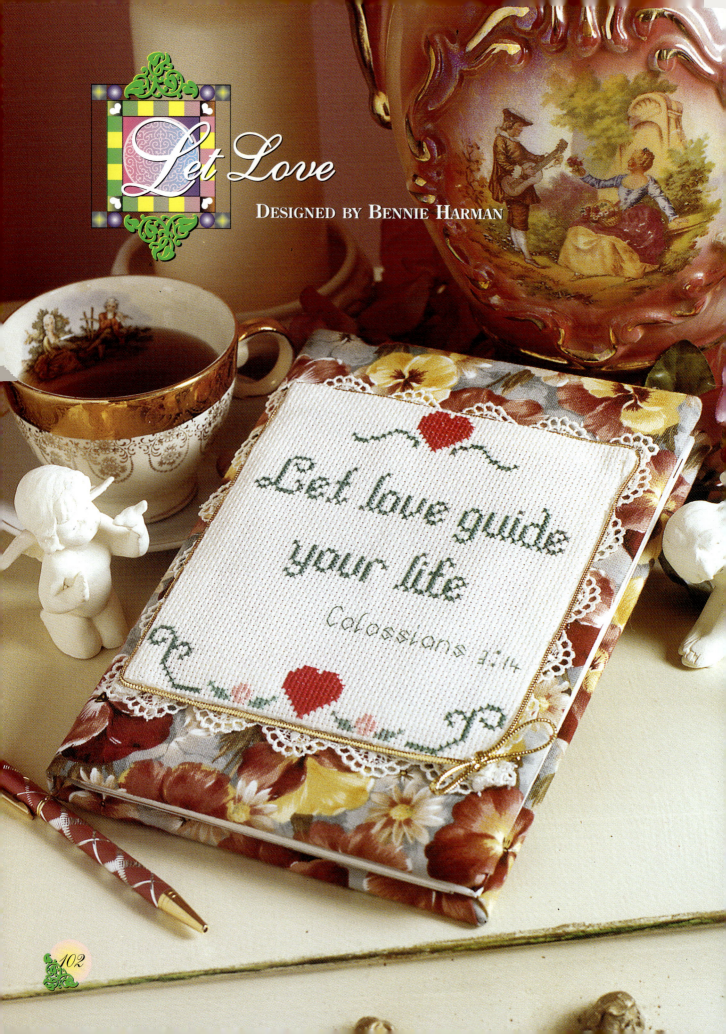

Materials

- 11" x 12" piece of antique white 14-count Aida
- 6" x 8½" fabric-covered address book
- Batting
- Lightweight cardboard
- ¾ yd. lace
- 1 yd. cord
- Craft glue or glue gun

Instructions

1: Center and stitch design, using two strands floss for Cross-Stitch and one strand floss for Backstitch and French Knot.

Note: From batting and cardboard, cut one each 5⅛" x 5⅝".

2: Center and mount design over batting and cardboard. Glue lace to back outside edges of mounted design. Glue cord around outside edges of mounted design; tie ends of cord into a bow at lower right corner as shown in photo.

3: Position and glue mounted design to front of address book as shown.

X	B'st	Fr	DMC	ANCHOR	J.&P. COATS	COLORS
■			#309	#42	#3284	Rose Deep
■	/	●	#501	#878	#6878	Sage Green Dk.
■			#502	#877	#6876	Sage Green Med.
■			#776	#24	#3281	Rose Pink Lt.

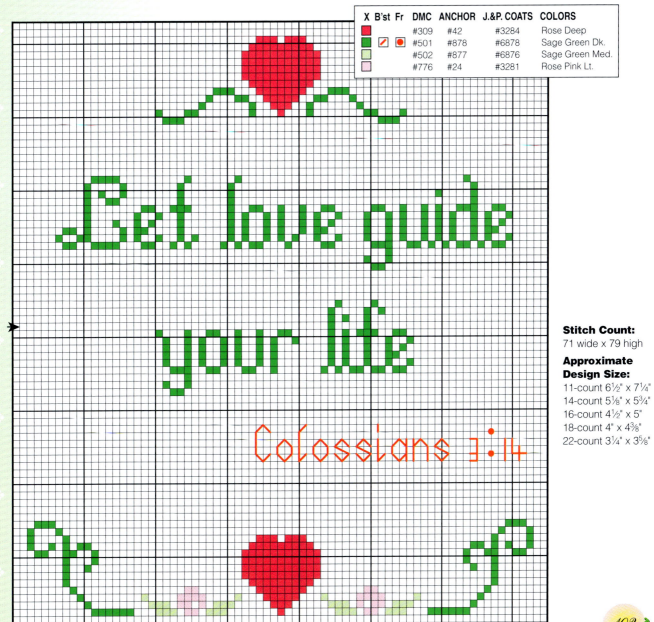

Stitch Count:
71 wide x 79 high

Approximate Design Size:
11-count 6½" x 7¼"
14-count 5⅛" x 5¾"
16-count 4½" x 5"
18-count 4" x 4⅜"
22-count 3¼" x 3⅝"

Simple Pleasures

Designed by Judith M. Chrispens

Materials

- 10" x 11" piece of coffee 28-count Jobelan®
- 8" x 10½" fabric-covered photo album
- Mounting board
- ¾ yd. pleated ruffle
- ½ yd. jute
- Craft glue or glue gun

Instructions

1: Center and stitch design, stitching over two threads and using two strands floss for Cross-Stitch and Backstitch of lettering and vines. Use two strands floss for French Knot and one strand floss for remaining Backstitch.

Note: From mounting board, cut one 4½" x 6".

2: Center and mount design over board. Glue ruffle to back outside edges of mounted design.

3: Position and glue mounted design to front of album as shown in photo. Tie jute into a bow; glue to top left corner of mounted design as shown.

Stitch Count:
48 wide x 72 high

Approximate Design Size:
11-count 4⅜" x 6⅝"
14-count 3½" x 5¼"
16-count 3" x 4½"
18-count 2¾" x 4"
22-count 2¼" x 3⅜"
28-count over two threads 3½" x 5¼"

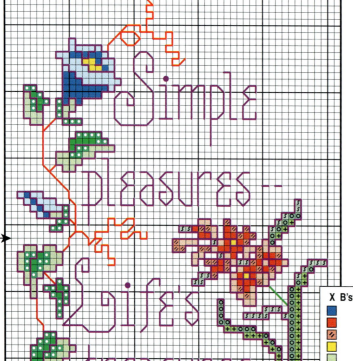

X	B'st	Fr	DMC	ANCHOR	J.&P. COATS	COLORS
■			#322	#978	#7978	Copen Blue
■			#350	#11	#3111	Coral Med.
▨			#351	#10	#3011	Coral
■			#445	#288	#2288	Lemon Lt.
■			#502	#877	#6876	Sage Green Med.
□			#561	#212	#6211	Jade Very Dk.
+			#562	#210	#6213	Jade Med.
O	✎		#563	#208	#6210	Jade Lt.
S			#564	#206	#6209	Jade Very Lt.
▨			#754	#1012	#2331	Peach Flesh Lt.
▨			#794	#175	#7977	Cornflower Blue Very Lt.
■	✎		#890	#218	#6021	Spruce Dk.
✎	●		#938	#381	#5381	Darkest Mahogany

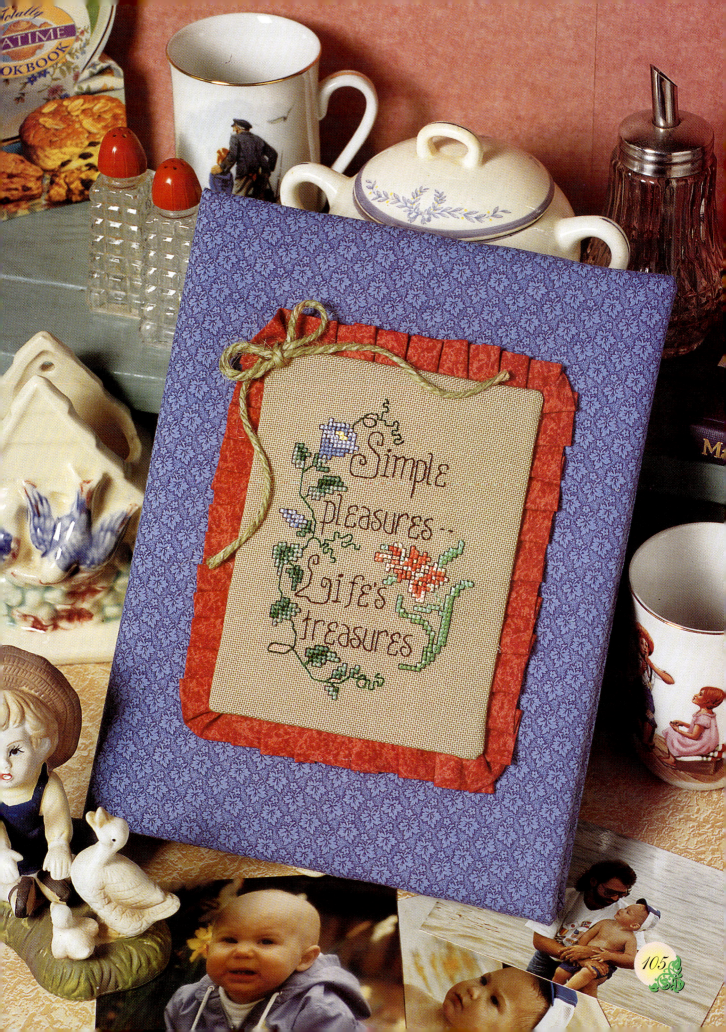

First of May

Designed by Ursula Michael

Materials

- 13" x 15" piece of white 28-count Annabelle®
- 1 yd. fabric
- ⅓ yd. contrasting fabric
- 12" x 16" pillow form

Instructions

1: Center and stitch design, stitching over two threads and using two strands floss or blending filament for Cross-Stitch. Use two strands floss for Backstitch and French Knot of lettering. Use one strand floss for remaining Backstitch.

Notes: Trim design to 9" x 11". From fabric, cut two 3¾" x 18" for A pieces, two 4¾" x 9" for B pieces, two 15" x 20" pieces for back and one 2" x 98" bias strip (piecing is necessary) for binding. From contrasting fabric, cut two 3¾" x 24" for band C pieces and two 3¾" x 20" for band D pieces. Use ½" seam allowance.

2: With right sides facing, sew design, A and B pieces together according to Front Assembly Diagram, forming center. With right sides facing, sew C and D band pieces to center according to Front Assembly Diagram, mitering corners to form front.

3: Hem one 20" edge of each back piece. Place one hemmed edge over the other, overlapping enough to create a 20" x 24" back with opening. Baste outside edges together; press.

4: With wrong sides facing, baste front and back together along outside edges, forming pillow. To form pillow pocket, sew ½" from inside edge of band pieces (see Front Assembly Diagram).

5: Press under ½" on each long edge of binding. With right sides facing, sew binding to front outside edges of pillow, folding corners as you sew. Fold binding to back and slip stitch in place. Insert pillow form.

Front Assembly Diagram

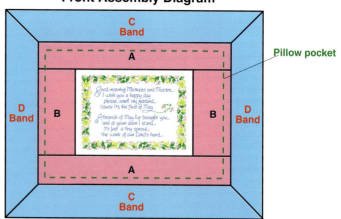

X	B'st	1/4x	Fr	DMC	ANCHOR	J.&P. COATS	KREINIK(BF)	COLORS
				#444	#290	#2290		Lemon Dk.
				#445	#288	#2288		Lemon Lt.
				#3345	#268	#6258		Ivy Green Dk.
				#3347	#266	#6010		Ivy Green
				#3348	#264	#6266		Apple Green
				#3608	#86	#4086		Plum Lt.
				#3809	#779	#7169		Wedgewood Med.
				#3819	#279	#6253		Moss Green Lt.
							#192	Pale Pink

Stitch Count:
130 wide x 91 high

Approximate Design Size:
11-count 11⅞" x 8⅜"
14-count 9⅜" x 6½"
16-count 8⅛" x 5¾"
18-count 7¼" x 5⅛"
22-count 6" x 4⅛"
28-count over two
  threads 9⅜" x 6½"

Help Me Remember

Designed by Marsha J. Coroso

Materials

- 12" x 13" piece of white 16-count Aida

Stitch Count:
110 wide x 88 high

Approximate Design Size:
11-count 10" x 8"
14-count 7⅞" x 6⅜"
16-count 6⅞" x 5½"
18-count 6⅛" x 5"
22-count 5" x 4"

Instructions

Note: If desired, initial and date work, as shown in photo.

Center and stitch design, using two strands floss for Cross-Stitch and one strand floss for Backstitch, Straight Stitch and French Knot.

My God is With Me

I may not understand today,
All the things that come my way,
But somewhere deep within my heart,
Burns so softly a heavenly spark.
His spirit moves me to kindle the flame,
Then the roaring fire burns again.
And when I think it all is lost,
I stop and think, remember the cross.
I carry my cross and you carry yours too,
With God as our Savior,
There's nothing we can't do.
Praise the Lord!

By Jannie Birch

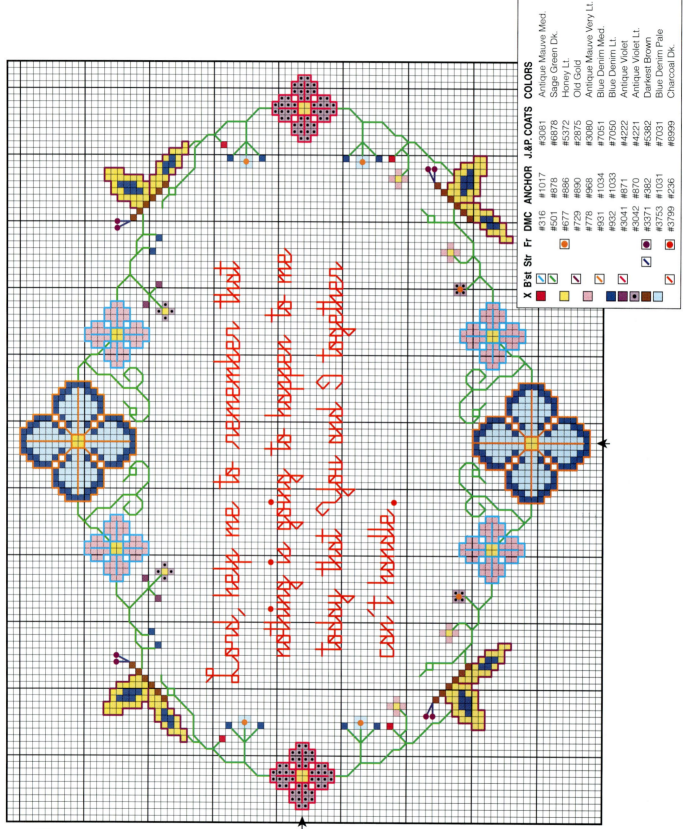

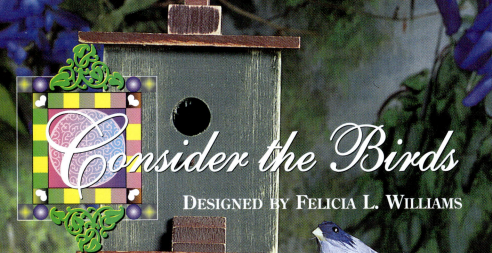

Consider the Birds

Designed by Felicia L. Williams

Consider the Birds

PHOTO ON PAGE 113

Materials

- 13" x 15" piece of light blue 14-count Aida

Instructions

Center and stitch design, using two strands floss for Cross-Stitch and one strand floss for Backstitch and French Knot.

Stitch Count:
128 wide x 101 high

Approximate Design Size:
11-count 11⅝" x 9¼"
14-count 9¼" x 7¼"
16-count 8" x 6⅜"
18-count 7⅛" x 5⅝"
22-count 5⅞" x 4⅝"

X	B'st	Fr	MADEIRA DECORA	DMC	ANCHOR	J.&P. COATS	COLORS
◇	/	●	#1400	#310	#403	#8403	Black
			#1412	#318	#399	#8511	Silver Med.
C			#1420	#722	#323	#2323	Orange Spice Lt.
ʌ			#1432	#3746	#1030	#7150	Blue Violet Med.
S			#1434	#3328	#1024	#3071	Salmon Dk.
■			#1435	#902	#897	#3083	Darkest Garnet
			#1437	#817	#13	#2335	Nasturtium
△			#1439	#304	#1006	#3410	Scarlet
◣			#1440	#414	#235	#8513	Silver Dk.
			#1441	#413	#401	#8514	Charcoal
			#1447	#954	#203	#6030	Seafoam Green Lt.
			#1449	#699	#923	#6228	Kelly Green Dk.
O			#1450	#702	#226	#6239	Kelly Green Lt.
▽			#1456	#801	#359	#5472	Coffee Brown Dk.
D			#1471	White	#2	#1001	White
I			#1475	#813	#161	#7161	Sky Blue Med.
⌐			#1478	#946	#332	#2332	Burnt Orange Dk.
>			#1482	#543	#933	#5533	Bone
▯			#1511	#340	#118	#7110	Blue Violet
—			#1514	#353	#8	#3006	Peach Flesh Med.
⊥			#1517	#760	#1022	#3069	Salmon
			#1520	#3713	#1020	#3068	Salmon Very Lt.
			#1522	#333	#119	#4301	Blue Violet Very Dk.
			#1523	#746	#275	#2275	Honey Pale
•			#1525	#725	#305	#2294	Topaz Med.
∪			#1526	#781	#309	#5309	Russet Med.
≷			#1533	#826	#161	#7180	Blue Med.
M			#1542	#839	#360	#5360	Pecan Dk.
∎			#1547	#321	#9046	#3500	Cherry Red
✕			#1549	#422	#373	#5350	Hazel Nut Lt.
/			#1555	#741	#304	#2314	Tangerine Dk.
⌐			#1558	#301	#1049	#5365	Cinnamon Lt.
	/		#1570	#319	#218	#6246	Spruce
T			#1574	#975	#355	#5356	Cinnamon Dk.
▮			#1575	#824	#164	#7182	Blue Very Dk.
+			#1578	#721	#324	#2324	Orange Spice Med.

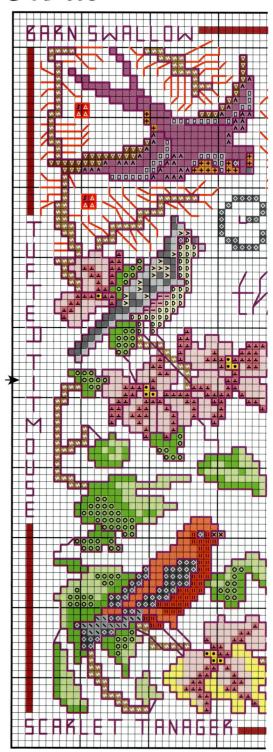

Advice to the Graduate

Designed by Linda Moore Wolf

Materials

- 13" x 14" piece of white 14-count Aida

Instructions

Selecting desired letters and numbers from Alphabet & Numbers graph, center and stitch design, using two strands floss or blending filament for Cross-Stitch. Use one strand floss for Backstitch and four strands floss for Straight Stitch.

Counsel for the Heart

I depart from my sanctuary,
The place that I call home.
To initiate a new beginning,
Yet I know I'm not alone.
The morals instilled from childhood,
Were placed by those who cared,
To teach me that life is not always easy,
And isn't always fair.
So I carry with me my Bible,
And your words within my heart,
The armor of God's salvation,
And Daddy's credit card.
Amen.
(p.s. thanks Dad)

By Jannie Birch

Stitch Count:
110 wide x 97 high

Approximate Design Size:
11-count 10" x 8⅞"
14-count 7⅞" x 7"
16-count 6⅞" x 6⅛"
18-count 6⅛" x 5⅜"
22-count 5" x 4½"

Alphabet & Numbers

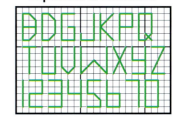

X	B'st	½x	¼x	¾x	Str	DMC	ANCHOR	J.&P. COATS	KREINIK(BF)	COLORS
						#469	#267	#6261		Avocado Green Med.
						#472	#253	#6253		Avocado Green Pale
						#727	#293	#2289		Topaz Lt.
						#743	#302	#2294		Tangerine Lt.
						#775	#128	#7031		Baby Blue
						#797	#132	#7023		Deep Blueberry
						#798	#131	#7022		Blueberry Dk.
						#799	#136	#7030		Blueberry Med.
						#839	#360	#5360		Pecan Dk.
						#840	#379	#5379		Pecan Med.
						#906	#256	#6256		Parrot Green Med. Dk.
						#937	#268	#6268		Black Avocado
						#972	#298	#2298		Tangerine Med.
									#002HL	Gold
									#051HL	Sapphire

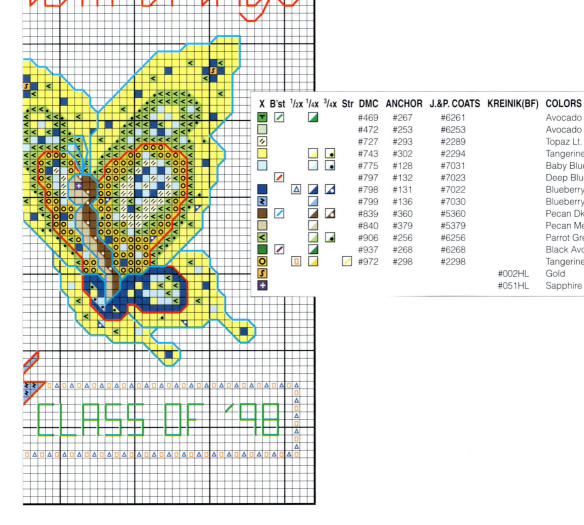

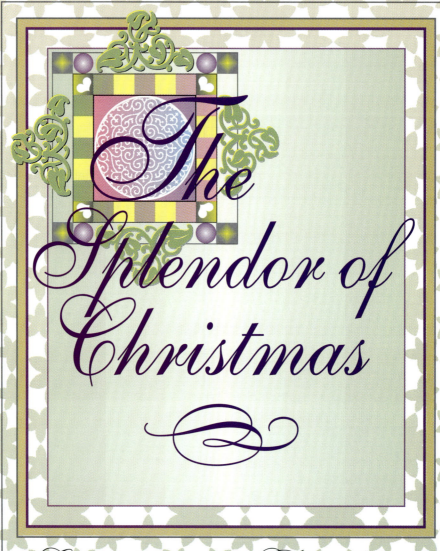

The Splendor of Christmas

Enchanting Delights

Chapter Six

Materials

- 16" x 16" piece of bone 28-count Lugana®
- 1 yd. fabric
- 1½ yds. ¼" piping
- 1½ yds. 3" lace
- 12" x 12" pillow form

Instructions

1: Center and stitch design, stitching over two threads and using two strands floss for Cross-Stitch and one strand floss for Backstitch.

Notes: Trim design to 13" x 13". From fabric, cut two 4" x 19" for A pieces, two 4" x 19" for B pieces and two 12" x 19" pieces for back. Use ½" seam allowance.

2: With right sides facing, sew to design first piping, then lace.

3: With right sides facing, sew design, A and B pieces together according to Front Assembly Diagram, mitering corners to form front.

4: Hem one 19" edge of each back piece. Place one hemmed edge over the other, overlapping enough to create a 19" x 19" back with opening. Baste outside edges together; press.

5: With right sides facing, sew front and back together. Trim seam and turn right sides out; press.

6: To form pillow pocket, sew around design close to inside edges of piping. Insert pillow form.

Twice or thrice had I loved thee
Before I knew thy face or name;
So in a voice, so in a shapeless flame
Angels affect us oft, and worshipped be.
Still, when to where thou wert I came,
Some lovely glorious nothing I did see. ...

From "Air and Angels"
by John Donne

X	B'st	1/4x	DMC	ANCHOR	J.&P. COATS	COLORS
			#208	#110	#4301	Lavender Dk.
			#210	#108	#4302	Lavender Lt.
			#211	#342	#4303	Lavender Pale
			#304	#1006	#3410	Scarlet
			#353	#8	#3006	Peach Flesh Med.
			#434	#310	#5000	Darkest Toast
			#436	#1045	#5943	Toast
			#601	#57	#3128	Cranberry Dk.
			#603	#62	#3153	Cranberry
			#644	#830	#5830	Beige Grey Lt.
			#666	#46	#3046	Geranium Dk.
			#676	#891	#2305	Honey
			#699	#923	#6228	Kelly Green Dk.
			#701	#227	#6226	Kelly Green Med.
			#703	#238	#6238	Parrot Green
			#725	#305	#2294	Topaz Med.
			#727	#293	#2289	Topaz Lt.
			#738	#361	#5375	Toast Very Lt.
			#746	#275	#2275	Honey Pale
			#776	#24	#3281	Rose Pink Lt.
			#783	#307	#5307	Topaz Very Dk.
			#818	#23	#3281	Antique Rose Very Lt.
			#822	#390	#5933	Beige Grey Very Lt.
			#826	#161	#7180	Blue Med.
			#827	#160	#7159	Sky Blue Lt.
			#828	#158	#7053	Larkspur Lt.
			#899	#52	#3282	Rose Pink Med.
			#909	#923	#6228	Green Dk.
			#910	#229	#6031	Darkest Seafoam Green
			#912	#209	#6266	Seafoam Green Dk.
		⊠	#948	#1011	#2331	Peach Flesh Very Lt.
			#966	#206	#6016	Pistachio Green Very Lt.
			#3705	#35	#3012	Carnation Dk.
	✓		#3799	#236	#8999	Charcoal Dk.
			White	#2	#1001	White

Front Assembly Diagram

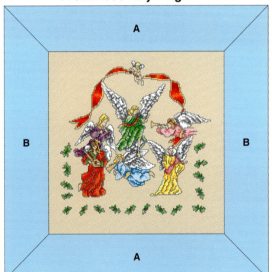

Stitch Count:
136 wide x 134 high

Approximate Design Size:
11-count 12 3/8" x 12 1/4"
14-count 9 3/4" x 9 5/8"
16-count 8 1/2" x 8 3/8"
18-count 7 5/8" x 7 1/2"
22-count 6 1/4" x 6 1/8"
28-count over two
  threads 9 3/4" x 9 5/8"

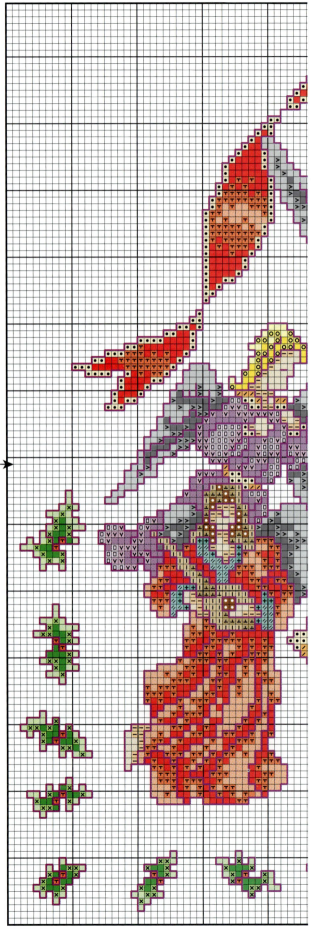

Country Ornaments

Designed by Linda Quinn

Materials

- Six 9" x 9" pieces of light oatmeal 14-count Fiddler's Lite
- ½ yd. fabric
- 1⅜ yds. piping
- Batting

Instructions

1: Center and stitch one design onto each piece of Fiddler's Lite, using two strands floss for Cross Stitch and one strand floss for Backstitch and French Knot.

Notes: Trim "Bow" design to 2½" x 4½" and remaining designs to 3½" x 3½". From fabric, cut four 3½" x 3½" for A pieces, two 2½" x 3" for B pieces, one 1½" x 8½" for C piece, two 2½" x 11" for D pieces, two 2½" x 10½" for E pieces and one 11" x 13½" piece for back. From batting, cut one 11" x 13½" piece. Use ½" seam allowance.

2: With right sides facing, sew designs, A, B, C, D and E pieces together according to Front

Front Assembly Diagram

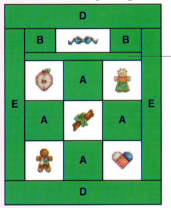

Heart
Stitch Count:
26 wide x 21 high

Approximate Design Size:
11-count 2⅜" x 2"
14-count 1⅞" x 1½"
16-count 1⅝" x 1⅜"
18-count 1½" x 1¼"
22-count 1¼" x 1"

Heart

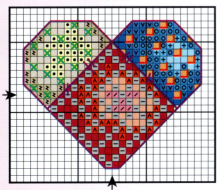

Bow

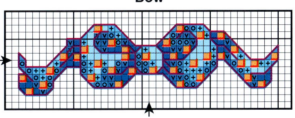

Bow
Stitch Count:
38 wide x 10 high

Approximate Design Size:
11-count 3½" x 1"
14-count 2¾" x ¾"
16-count 1⅜" x ⅝"
18-count 2⅜" x ⅝"
22-count 1¾" x ½"

X	B'st	¼x	Fr	DMC	ANCHOR	J.&P. COATS	COLORS
■		◪		#311	#148	#7980	Indigo Blue Dk.
V		◪		#312	#979	#7979	Azure Blue Dk.
T	◪	◪		#320	#215	#6017	Pistachio Green Med.
/		◪		#326	#59	#3401	Dk. Rose
O		◪		#334	#977	#7978	Delft Blue Dk.
■		◪		#367	#217	#6018	Pistachio Green Dk.
W		◪		#368	#214	#6016	Pistachio Green Lt.
		◪		#369	#1043	#6015	Pistachio Green Pale
X		◪		#434	#310	#5000	Darkest Toast
	◪	◪		#436	#1045	#5943	Toast
Z		◪		#738	#361	#5375	Toast Very Lt.
		◪		#739	#387	#5369	Toast Pale
■		◪		#801	#359	#5472	Coffee Brown Dk.
■		◪		#814	#45	#3044	Garnet Very Dk.
∧		◪		#815	#43	#3000	Garnet Dk.
		◪		#816	#20	#3021	Garnet Med.
●		◪		#890	#218	#6021	Spruce Dk.
+		◪		#938	#381	#5381	Darkest Mahogany
■		◪		#3325	#129	#7976	Delft Blue
	◪		●	#3371	#382	#5382	Darkest Brown
+		◪		#3755	#140	#7977	Delft Blue Med.
–		◪		White	#2	#1001	White
●		◪		Ecru	#387	#1002	Ecru

Assembly Diagram, forming front. With right sides facing, sew piping to outside edges of front. Baste batting to wrong side of front. With right sides facing, sew front and back together, leaving an opening. Turn right sides out; slip stitch opening closed.

3: Sewing through all thicknesses, sew around edge of each Fiddler's Lite piece.

Apple

Apple Stitch Count:
22 wide x 29 high

Approximate Design Size:
11-count 2" x 2⅝"
14-count 1⅝" x 2⅛"
16-count 1⅜" x 1⅞"
18-count 1¼" x 1⅝"
22-count 1" x 1⅜"

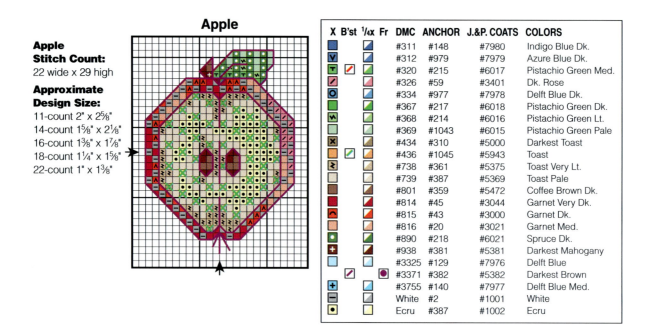

X	B'st	¼x	Fr	DMC	ANCHOR	J.&P. COATS	COLORS
				#311	#148	#7980	Indigo Blue Dk.
				#312	#979	#7979	Azure Blue Dk.
				#320	#215	#6017	Pistachio Green Med.
				#326	#59	#3401	Dk. Rose
				#334	#977	#7978	Delft Blue Dk.
				#367	#217	#6018	Pistachio Green Dk.
				#368	#214	#6016	Pistachio Green Lt.
				#369	#1043	#6015	Pistachio Green Pale
				#434	#310	#5000	Darkest Toast
				#436	#1045	#5943	Toast
				#738	#361	#5375	Toast Very Lt.
				#739	#387	#5369	Toast Pale
				#801	#359	#5472	Coffee Brown Dk.
				#814	#45	#3044	Garnet Very Dk.
				#815	#43	#3000	Garnet Dk.
				#816	#20	#3021	Garnet Med.
				#890	#218	#6021	Spruce Dk.
				#938	#381	#5381	Darkest Mahogany
				#3325	#129	#7976	Delft Blue
				#3371	#382	#5382	Darkest Brown
				#3755	#140	#7977	Delft Blue Med.
				White	#2	#1001	White
				Ecru	#387	#1002	Ecru

Cinnamon Stitch Count:
27 wide x 27 high

Approximate Design Size:
11-count 2½" x 2½"
14-count 2" x 2"
16-count 1¾" x 1¾"
18-count 1½" x 1½"
22-count 1¼" x 1¼"

Cinnamon

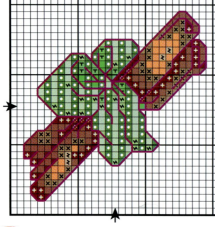

Gingerbread Boy

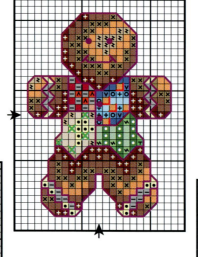

Gingerbread Boy Stitch Count:
21 wide x 29 high

Approximate Design Size:
11-count 2" x 2⅝"
14-count 1½" x 2⅛"
16-count 1⅜" x 1⅞"
18-count 1¼" x 1⅝"
22-count 1" x 1⅜"

Gingerbread Girl

Gingerbread Girl Stitch Count:
21 wide x 31 high

Approximate Design Size:
11-count 2" x 2⅞"
14-count 1½" x 2¼"
16-count 1⅜" x 2"
18-count 1¼" x 1¾"
22-count 1" x 1½"

Christmas Bear
DESIGNED BY MIKE VICKERY

Christmas Bear

PHOTO ON PAGE 135

Materials

- 12" x 20" piece of silver blue 28-count Linen
- ⅓ yd. fabric
- Batting
- 1¾ yds. ribbon
- 10 jingle bells of choice

Instructions

1: Center and stitch design, stitching over two threads and using two strands floss for Cross-Stitch and one strand floss for Backstitch.

Notes: Trim design to 10" x 18" for front. From fabric, cut one 10" x 18" piece for back. From batting, cut one 10" x 18" piece. Use ½" seam allowance.

2: Baste batting to wrong side of front. With right sides facing, sew front and back together, leaving an

opening. Turn right sides out; slip stitch opening closed. Sewing through all thicknesses, sew around design edges. Tack cord around outside edges as shown in photo.

3: Decorate with ribbon and jingle bells as shown or as desired.

Stitch Count:
80 wide x 200 high

Approximate Design Size:
11-count 7⅜" x 18¼"
14-count 5¾" x 14⅜"
16-count 5" x 12½"
18-count 4½" x 11⅛"
22-count 3⅝" x 9⅛"
28-count over two
  threads 5¾" x 14⅜"

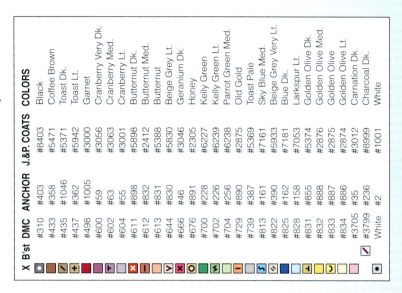

X	B'st	DMC	ANCHOR	J.&P. COATS	COLORS
		#310	#403	#8403	Black
		#433	#358	#5471	Coffee Brown
		#435	#1046	#5371	Toast Dk.
		#437	#362	#5942	Toast Lt.
		#498	#1005	#3000	Garnet
		#600	#59	#3056	Cranberry Very Dk.
		#602	#63	#3063	Cranberry Med.
		#604	#55	#3001	Cranberry Lt.
		#611	#898	#5898	Butternut Dk.
		#612	#832	#2412	Butternut Med.
		#613	#831	#5388	Butternut
		#644	#830	#5830	Beige Grey Lt.
		#666	#46	#3046	Geranium Dk.
		#676	#891	#2305	Honey
		#700	#228	#6227	Kelly Green
		#702	#226	#6239	Kelly Green Lt.
		#704	#256	#6238	Parrot Green Med.
		#729	#890	#2875	Old Gold
		#739	#387	#5369	Toast Pale
		#813	#161	#7161	Sky Blue Med.
		#822	#390	#5933	Beige Grey Very Lt.
		#825	#162	#7181	Blue Dk.
		#828	#158	#7053	Larkspur Lt.
		#831	#855	#5374	Golden Olive Dk.
		#832	#888	#2876	Golden Olive Med.
		#833	#887	#2875	Golden Olive
		#834	#886	#2874	Golden Olive Lt.
		#3705	#35	#3012	Carnation Dk.
		#3799	#236	#8999	Charcoal Dk.
		White	#2	#1001	White

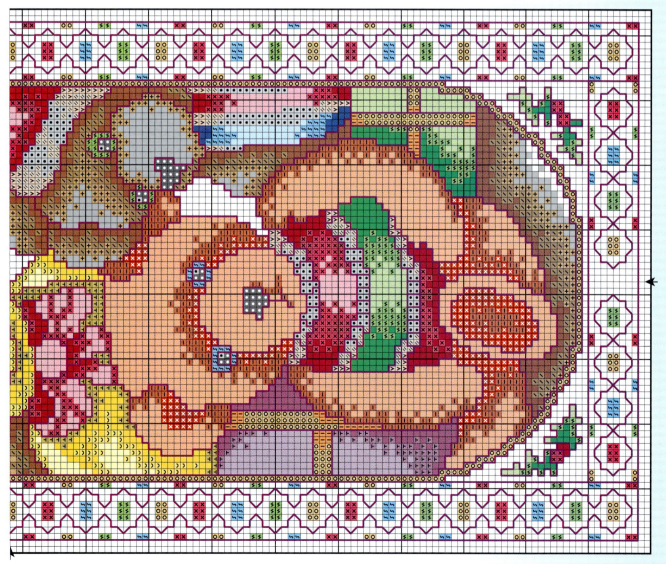

Materials

- 16" x 19" piece of bone 28-count Lugana®

Stitch Count:
179 wide x 135 high

Approximate Design Size:
11-count 16⅜" x 12⅜"
14-count 12⅞" x 9¾"
16-count 11¾" x 8½"
18-count 10" x 7½"
22-count 8⅛" x 6⅛"
28-count over two threads 12⅞" x 9¾"

Instructions

Center and stitch design, stitching over two threads and using two strands floss for Cross-Stitch, Backstitch of lettering and French Knot. Use three strands floss for Straight Stitch and one strand floss for remaining Backstitch.

X	B'st	¼x	¾x	Str	Fr	DMC	ANCHOR	J.&P. COATS	COLORS
						#300	#352	#5349	Mahogany Very Dk.
						#319	#218	#6246	Spruce
						#320	#215	#6017	Pistachio Green Med.
						#367	#217	#6018	Pistachio Green Dk.
						#368	#214	#6016	Pistachio Green Lt.
						#642	#392	#5832	Beige Grey Dk.
						#676	#891	#2305	Honey
						#677	#886	#5372	Honey Lt.
						#680	#901	#2876	Old Gold Dk.
						#729	#890	#2875	Old Gold
						#754	#1012	#3868	Peach Flesh Lt.
						#761	#1021	#3068	Salmon Lt.
						#762	#234	#8510	Silver Very Lt.
						#801	#359	#5472	Coffee Brown
						#822	#390	#5933	Beige Grey Very Lt.
						#898	#360	#5476	Coffee Brown Very Dk.
						#930	#1035	#7052	Blue Denim Dk.
						#931	#1034	#7051	Blue Denim Med.
						#932	#1033	#7050	Blue Denim Lt.
						#948	#1011	#2331	Peach Flesh Very Lt.
						#3031	#360	#5477	Coffee Brown Dk.
						#3033	#391	#5831	Beige Grey Pale
						#3072	#847	#6005	Pearl Grey
						#3685	#1028	#3090	Darkest Mauve
						#3687	#68	#3088	Mauve Med.
						#3688	#66	#3087	Mauve
						#3752	#1032	#7876	Blue Denim Very Lt.
						#3779	#868	#3868	Terra Cotta Very Lt.
						#3803	#69	#3089	Mauve Dk.
						White	#2	#1001	White
						Ecru	#387	#1002	Ecru

I ride with you
n your sleigh of red?
you feel that I should be
asleep inside my bed.
   I must admit, a cozy nap
      upon this Christmas Eve,
   is very tempting Santa dear.
How soon do you plan to leave?
The more I think about a nap,
   the more I think I'll stay,
   and curl up inside my bed
      to sleep 'til
         Christmas Day.

Santa

Designed by Mike Vickery

Materials

- 12" x 18" piece of white 28-count Monaco
- 1 yd. fabric
- Batting
- 2 yds. ½" decorative trim
- 1⅜ yds. ¾" decorative trim

Instructions

1: Center and stitch design, stitching over two threads and using two strands floss for Cross-Stitch and one strand floss for Backstitch.

Notes: Trim design to 8" x 13¾". From fabric, cut two 13¾" x 19" pieces for front and back. From batting, cut one 13¾" x 19" piece. Use ½" seam allowance.

2: With right sides facing, sew ½" decorative trim to outside edges of front. Baste batting to wrong side of front. For wall hanging, with right sides facing, sew front and back together, leaving an opening. Turn right sides out; slip stitch opening closed.

3: Press under ¼" hem around edges of design. Sew ¾" decorative trim to front outside edges of design, forming appliqué. Sewing through all thicknesses, position and sew appliqué to wall hanging as shown in photo.

Down the chimney, St. Nicholas came with a bound. He was dressed all in fur from head to his foot. And his clothes were all tarnished with ashes and soot; A bundle of toys he had flung on his back…

From "The Night Before Christmas" by Clement Clark Moore

Stitch Count:
80 wide x 169 high

Approximate Design Size:
11-count 7⅜" x 15⅜"
14-count 5¾" x 12⅛"
16-count 5" x 10⅝"
18-count 4½" x 9⅜"
22-count 3⅝" x 7¾"
28-count over two threads 5¾" x 12⅛"

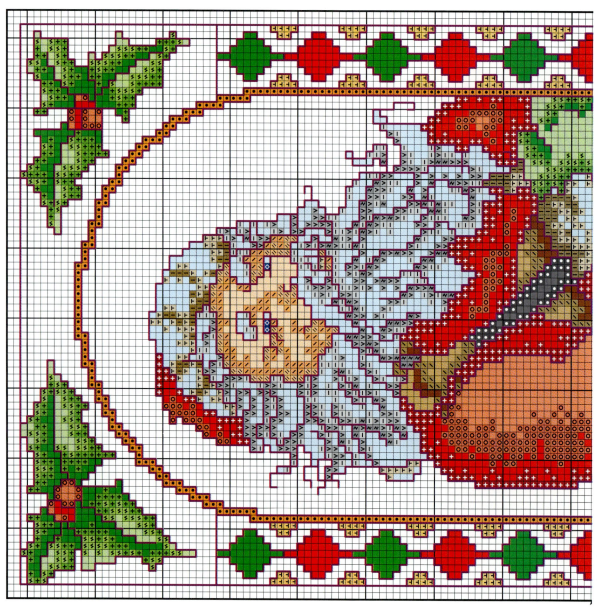

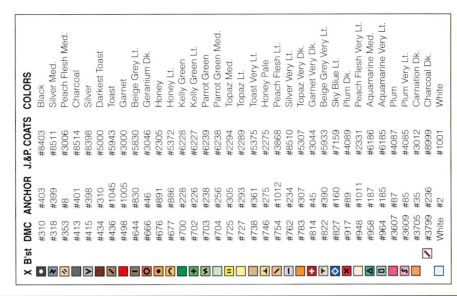
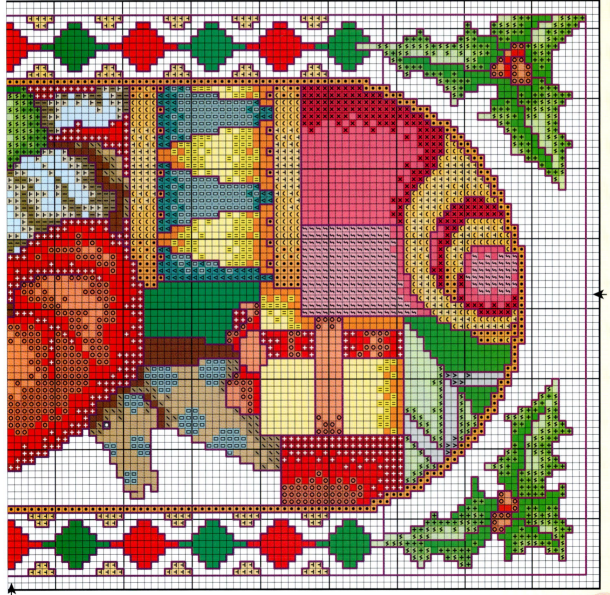

Mr. Snowman

Designed by Linda Quinn

X	B'st	¼x	Fr	DMC	ANCHOR	J.&P. COATS	COLORS
■		◢	●	#310	#403	#8403	Black
■	◢	◢		#312	#979	#7979	Azure Blue Dk.
◉				#319	#218	#6246	Spruce
✕				#320	#215	#6017	Pistachio Green Med.
✚				#322	#978	#7978	Copen Blue
◪				#322	#978	#7978	Copen Blue held with
				#434	#310	#5000	Darkest Toast
■		◢		#326	#59	#3401	Dk. Rose
◆	◢	◢		#334	#977	#7977	Delft Blue Dk.
◢				#334	#977	#7977	Delft Blue Dk. held with
				#436	#1045	#5943	Toast
⚐				#335	#38	#3283	Rose Pink Dk.
■		◢		#340	#118	#7110	Blue Violet
⊤		◢		#341	#117	#7005	Blue Violet Lt.
◪				#341	#117	#7005	Blue Violet Lt. held with
				#775	#128	#7031	Baby Blue
⚡				#367	#217	#6018	Pistachio Green Dk.
⌒				#368	#214	#6016	Pistachio Green Lt.
◢				#413	#401	#8514	Charcoal
◣				#414	#235	#8513	Silver Dk.
■		◢		#415	#398	#8398	Silver
✚		◢		#433	#358	#5471	Coffee Brown
⚐		◢		#434	#310	#5000	Darkest Toast
⚑		◢		#435	#1046	#5371	Toast Dk.
▦				#436	#1045	#5943	Toast
◧		◢		#738	#361	#5375	Toast Very Lt. held with
				#3755	#140	#7976	Delft Blue Med.
□				#739	#387	#5369	Toast Pale
⤹				#739	#387	#5369	Toast Pale held with
				#775	#128	#7031	Baby Blue
□			●	#742	#303	#2302	Tangerine
▷				#743	#302	#2294	Tangerine Lt.
□		◢		#775	#128	#7031	Baby Blue
□				#776	#24	#3281	Rose Pink Lt.
■				#801	#359	#5472	Coffee Brown Dk.
◉	◢	◢		#815	#43	#3000	Garnet Dk.
⌒	◢			#890	#683	#6021	Spruce Dk.
✕		◢		#895	#1044	#6246	Darkest Ivy Green
✚				#904	#258	#6258	Darkest Parrot Green
▽		◢		#905	#257	#6266	Parrot Green Dk.
◻				#907	#255	#6001	Parrot Green Lt.
◁	◢			#938	#381	#5381	Darkest Mahogany
♡				#950	#4146	#3146	Fawn
Ξ				#976	#1001	#2308	Golden Brown Med.
⊂		◢		#977	#1002	#2306	Golden Brown
⋀		◢		#986	#246	#6268	Pistachio Green Ultra Dk.
✕				#3325	#129	#7020	Delft Blue
▲				#3325	#129	#7020	Delft Blue held with
				#3747	#120	#7004	Blue Violet Very Lt.
□				#3326	#36	#3126	Rose Pink
	◢			#3371	#382	#5382	Darkest Brown
□				#3747	#120	#7004	Blue Violet Very Lt.
▽				#3755	#140	#7976	Delft Blue Med.
⬤				#3756	#1037	#7975	Baby Blue Very Lt.
◨		◢	●	#3770	#1009	#3334	Cream Lt.
□		◢		#3815	#877	#6876	Celdon Green Dk.
◉				#3816	#876	#6879	Celdon Green
□				#3817	#875	#6875	Celdon Green Lt.
▲				#3826	#349	#5349	Golden Brown Dk.
□				#3827	#311	#5351	Golden Brown Lt.
□			●	White	#2	#1001	White

Materials

- 12" x 13" piece of white 14-count Aida

Instructions

Center and stitch design, using two strands floss for Cross-Stitch and French Knot. Use one strand floss for Backstitch.

Stitch Count:
80 wide x 100 high

Approximate Design Size:
11-count 7⅜" x 9⅛"
14-count 5¾" x 7¼"
16-count 5" x 6¼"
18-count 4½" x 5⅝"
22-count 3⅝" x 4⅝"

Blow, blow, thou winter wind,
Thou are not so unkind
As man's ingratitude;
Thy tooth is not so keen
Because thou art not seen,…

From " Blow, blow, thou
winter wind"
by William Shakespeare

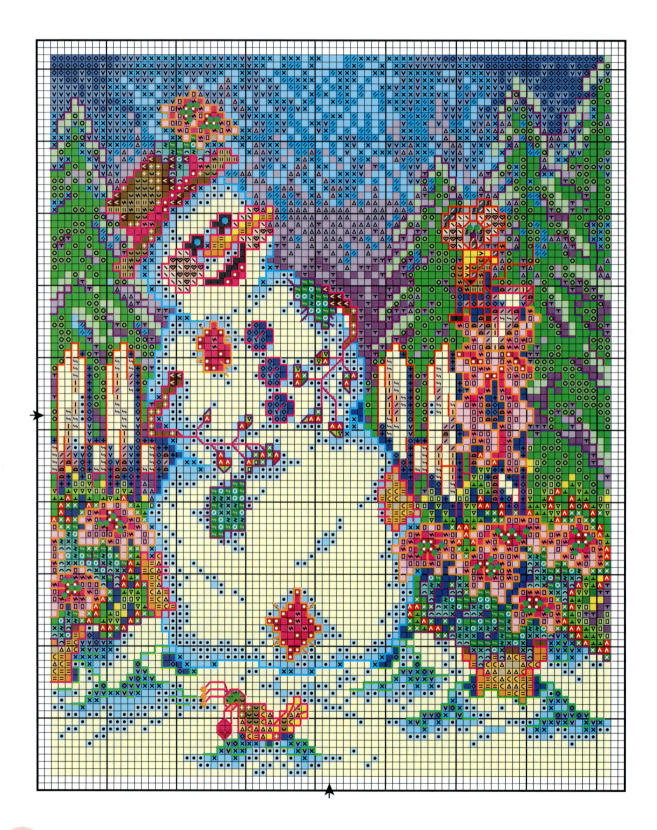

Flying Angel

PHOTO ON PAGE 149

Materials

- 9" x 13" piece of antique white 14-count Aida
- Fabric-covered card box of choice
- Foam core board
- ⅝ yd. ⅝" lace
- Craft glue or glue gun

Instructions

1: Center and stitch design, using three strands floss for Cross-Stitch and Running Stitch. Use one strand floss for Backstitch.

Note: From foam core board, cut one 3⅝" x 7¼".

2: Center and mount design over board. Glue lace around outside edges of mounted design.

3: Position and glue mounted design to front of card box as shown in photo.

X	B'st	Run	DMC	ANCHOR	J.&P. COATS	COLORS
■			#320	#215	#6017	Pistachio Green Med.
◉			#353	#8	#3006	Peach Flesh Med.
■			#434	#310	#5000	Darkest Toast
+			#597	#168	#7168	Wedgewood Lt.
■			#676	#891	#2305	Honey
■			#761	#1021	#3068	Salmon Lt.
	✎		#842	#368	#5933	Pecan Cream
■			#3712	#1023	#3071	Salmon Med.
		✎	#3799	#236	#8999	Charcoal Dk.
■			#3810	#168	#7226	Wedgewood
■			#3811	#928	#7053	Wedgewood Very Pale
○			Ecru	#387	#1002	Ecru

Stitch Count:
93 wide x 43 high

Approximate Design Size:
11-count 8½" x 4"
14-count 6¾" x 3⅛"
16-count 5⅞" x 2¾"
18-count 5¼" x 2⅜"
22-count 4¼" x 2"

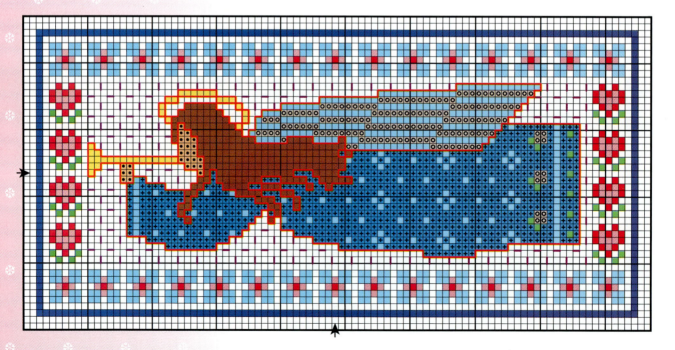

Tools of the Stitcher

Fabrics

Most counted cross-stitch projects are worked on evenweave fabrics made especially for counted thread embroidery. These fabrics have vertical and horizontal threads of uniform thickness and spacing. Aida cloth is a favorite of beginning stitchers because its weave forms distinctive squares in the fabric, which makes placing stitches easy. To determine a fabric's thread count, count the number of threads per inch of fabric.

Linen is made from fibers of the flax plant and is strong and durable. Its lasting quality makes it the perfect choice for heirloom projects. Linen is available in a range of muted colors and stitch counts.

In addition to evenweave fabrics, many stitchers enjoy using waste canvas and perforated paper. Waste canvas is basted to clothing or other fabric, forming a grid for stitching which is later removed. Perforated paper has holes evenly spaced for 14 stitches per inch.

Needles

Cross-stitch needles should have elongated eyes and blunt points. They should slip easily between the threads of the fabric, but should not pierce the fabric. The most common sizes used for cross-stitching are size 24 or 26. The ideal needle size is just small enough to slip easily through your fabric. Some stitchers prefer to use a slightly smaller needle for backstitching. When stitching on waste canvas, use a sharp needle.

Hoops, Frames & Scissors

Hoops can be round or oval and come in many sizes. The three main types are plastic, spring-tension and wooden. Frames are easier on the fabric than hoops and come in many sizes and shapes. Once fabric is mounted it doesn't have to be removed until stitching is complete, saving fabric from excessive handling.

Small, sharp scissors are essential for cutting floss and removing mistakes. For cutting fabrics, invest in a top-quality pair of medium-sized sewing scissors. To keep them in top form, use these scissors only for cutting fabrics and floss.

Stitching Threads

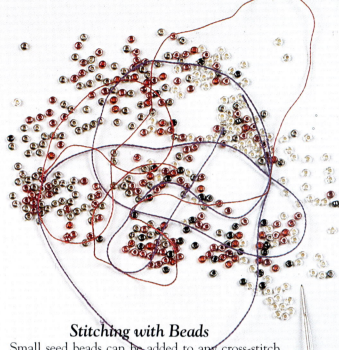

Today's cross-stitcher can achieve a vast array of effects in texture, color and shine. In addition to the perennial favorite, six-strand floss, stitchers can choose from sparkling metallics, shiny rayons, silks, narrow ribbon threads and much more.

Six-Strand Floss
Six-strand floss comes in a variety of colors and is available in metallics, silk and rayon as well as cotton. Most projects are worked using two or three strands of floss for cross-stitches and one or two strands for backstitches. For ease of stitching and to prevent wear on fibers, use lengths no longer than 18".

Pearl Cotton
Pearl cotton is available in #3, #5 and #8, with #3 being the thickest. The plies of pearl cotton will not separate, and for most stitching one strand is used. Pearl cotton has a lustrous sheen.

Flower & Ribbon Threads
Flower thread has a tight twist and comes in many soft colors. It is heavier than one ply of six-strand floss – one strand of flower thread equals two strands of floss. Ribbon thread is a narrow ribbon especially created for stitching. It comes in a large number of colors in satin as well as metallic finishes.

Blending Filament & Metallic Braid
Blending filament is a fine, shiny fiber that can be used alone or combined with floss or other thread. Knotting the blending filament on the needle with a slipknot is recommended for control.

Metallic braid is a braided metallic fiber, usually used single-ply. Thread this fiber just as you would any other fiber. Use short lengths, about 15", to keep the fiber from fraying.

Stitching with Beads
Small seed beads can be added to any cross-stitch design, using one bead per stitch. Knot thread at beginning of beaded section for security, especially if you are adding beads to clothing. The bead should lie in the same direction as the top half of cross-stitches.

Bead Attachment
Use one strand floss to secure beads. Bring beading needle up from back of work, leaving 2" length of thread hanging; do not knot (end will be secured between stitches as you work.) Thread bead on needle; complete stitch.

Do not skip over more than two stitches or spaces without first securing thread, or last bead will be loose. To secure, weave thread into several stitches on back of work. Follow graph to work design, using one bead per stitch.

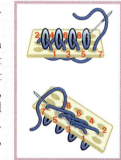

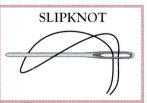
SLIPKNOT

Before You Begin

Assemble fabric, floss, pattern and tools. Familiarize yourself with the graph, color key and instructions before beginning.

Preparing Fabric

Before you stitch, decide how large to cut fabric. If you are making a pillow or other design which requires a large unstitched area, be sure to leave plenty of fabric. If you are making a small project, leave at least 3" around all edges of design. Determine the design area size by using this formula: number of stitches across design area divided by the number of threads per inch of fabric equals size of fabric in inches. Measure fabric, then cut evenly along horizontal and vertical threads.

Press out folds. To prevent raveling, hand overcast or machine zigzag fabric edges. Find center of fabric by folding horizontally and vertically, and mark with a small stitch.

Reading Graphs

Cross-stitch graphs or charts are made up of colors and symbols to tell you the exact color, type and placement of each stitch. Each square represents the area for one complete cross-stitch. Next to each graph, there is a key with information about stitches and floss colors represented by the graph's colors and symbols.

Color keys have abbreviated headings for cross-stitch (x), one-half cross-stitch (½x), quarter cross-stitch (¼x), three-quarter cross-stitch (¾x), back-stitch (B'st), French knot (Fr), lazy daisy stitch (LzD) and straight stitch (Str). Some graphs are so large they must be divided for printing.

Preparing Floss

The six strands of floss are easily separated, and the number of strands used is given in instructions. Cut strands in 14"-18" lengths. When separating floss, always separate all six strands, then recombine the number of strands needed. To make floss separating easier, run cut length across a damp sponge. To prevent floss from tangling, run cut length through a fabric-softener dryer sheet before separating and threading needle. To colorfast red floss tones, which sometimes bleed, hold floss under running water until water runs clear. Allow to air dry.

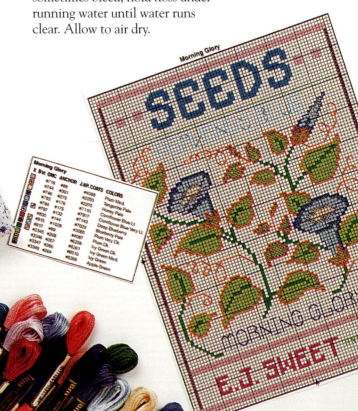

Stitching Techniques

Beginning & Ending a Thread

Try these methods for beginning a thread, then decide which one is best for you.

1: Securing the thread: Start by pulling needle through fabric back to front, leaving about 1" behind fabric. Hold this end with fingers as you begin stitching, and work over end with your first few stitches. After work is in progress, weave end through the back of a few stitches.

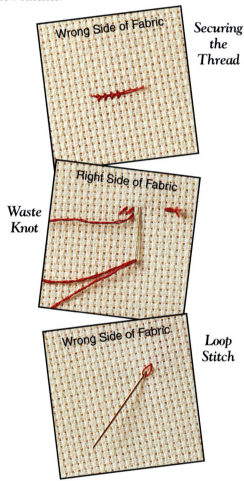

2: Waste knot: Make a knot in end of floss and pull needle through fabric front to back several squares over from where your first cross-stitch will be. Come up at first stitch and stitch first few stitches over floss end. Clip knot.

3: Loop stitch: This method can only be used for even numbers of strands. Cut strands twice the normal length, then take half the number of strands needed and fold in half. Insert loose ends in needle and bring needle up from back at first stitch, leaving loop underneath. Take needle down through fabric and through loop; pull to secure.

For even stitches, keep a consistent tension on your thread, and pull thread and needle completely through fabric with each stab of the needle. Make all the top crosses on your cross-stitches face the same direction. To finish a thread, run the needle under the back side of several stitches and clip. Threads carried across the back of unworked areas may show through to the front, so do not carry threads.

Master Stitchery

Work will be neater if you always try to make each stitch by coming up in an unoccupied hole and going down in an occupied hole.

The sewing method is preferred for stitching on linen and some other even-weaves, but can also be used on Aida. Stitches are made as in hand sewing with needle going from front to back to front of fabric in one motion. All work is done from the front of the fabric. When stitching with the sewing method, it is important not to pull thread too tightly or stitches will become distorted. Stitching on linen is prettiest with the sewing method, using no hoop. If you use a hoop or frame when using the sewing method with Aida, keep in mind that fabric cannot be pulled taut. There must be "give" in the fabric in order for needle to slip in and out easily.

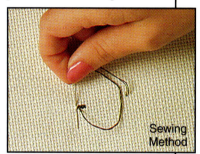

In the stab method, needle and floss are taken completely through fabric twice with each stitch. For the first half of the stitch, bring needle up and pull thread completely through fabric to the front. Then take needle down and reach underneath and pull completely through to bottom.

Working on Evenweave

When working on linen or other evenweave fabric, keep needle on right side of fabric, taking needle front to back to front with each stitch. Work over two threads, placing the beginning and end of the bottom half of the first Cross-Stitch where a vertical thread crosses a horizontal thread.

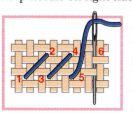

Cleaning Your Needlework

Careful washing, pressing and sometimes blocking help preserve and protect your stitched piece. After stitching is complete, a gentle washing will remove surface dirt, hoop marks and hand oils that have accumulated on your fabric while stitching. Even if a piece looks clean, it's always a good idea to give it a nice cleaning before finishing. Never press your work before cleaning, as this only serves to set those hoop marks and soils that are best removed.

Using a gentle soap such as baby shampoo or gentle white dishwashing liquid and a large, clean bowl, make a solution of cool, sudsy water. If you use a handwash product, make sure the one you choose contains no chlorine bleach. Fill another bowl or sink with plain cool water for rinsing.

Soak your stitched piece in sudsy water for five to ten minutes. Then gently and without rubbing or twisting, squeeze suds through fabric several times. Dip piece several times in fresh cool water until no suds remain.

On rare occasions floss colors will run or fade slightly. When this happens, continue to rinse in cool water until water becomes perfectly clear. Remove fabric from water and lay on a soft, white towel. Never twist or wring your work. Blot excess water away and roll the piece up in the towel, pressing gently.

Never allow a freshly washed piece of embroidery to air dry. Instead, remove the damp piece from the towel and place face down on a fresh, dry white towel. To prevent color stains, it's important to keep the stitched piece flat, not allowing stitched areas to touch each other or other areas of the fabric. Make sure the edges of fabric are in straight lines and even. To be sure fabric edges are straight when pressing dry, use a ruler or T-square to check edges. Wash towel several times before using it to block cross-stitch, and use it only for this purpose.

After edges are aligned and fabric is perfectly smooth, cover the back of the stitched piece with a pressing cloth, cotton diaper or other lightweight white cotton cloth. Press dry with a dry iron set on a high permanent press or cotton setting, depending on fabric content. Allow stitchery to lie in this position several hours. Machine drying is acceptable after use for items like towels and kitchen accessories, but your work will be prettier and smoother if you give these items a careful pressing the first time.

156

Framing & Mounting

Shopping for Frames

When you shop for a frame, take the stitchery along with you and compare several frame and mat styles. Keep in mind the "feeling" of your stitched piece when choosing a frame. For example, an exquisite damask piece stitched with metallics and silk threads might need an ornate gold frame, while a primitive sampler stitched on dirty linen with flower thread would need a simpler, perhaps wooden frame.

Mounting

Cross-stitch pieces can be mounted on mat board, white cardboard, special padded or unpadded mounting boards designed specifically for needlework, or special acid-free mat board available from art supply stores. Acid-free framing materials are the best choice for projects you wish to keep well-preserved for future generations. If you prefer a padded look, cut quilt batting to fit mounting board.

Center blocked stitchery over mounting board of choice with quilt batting between, if desired. Leaving 1½" to 3" around all edges, trim excess fabric away along straight grain.

Mounting boards made for needlework have self-stick surfaces and require no pins. When using these products, lift and smooth needlework onto board until work is taut and edges are smooth and even. Turn board face down and smooth fabric to back, mitering corners.

Pins are required for other mounting boards. With design face up, keeping fabric straight and taut, insert a pin through fabric and edge of mounting board at the center of each side. Turn piece face down and smooth excess fabric to back, mitering corners.

There are several methods for securing fabric edges. Edges may be glued to mat board with liquid fabric glue or fabric glue stick. If mat board is thick, fabric may be stapled.

Mats & Glass

Pre-cut mats are available in many sizes and colors to fit standard-size frames. Custom mats are available in an even wider variety of colors, textures and materials. Using glass over cross-stitch is a matter of personal preference, but is generally discouraged. Moisture can collect behind glass and rest on fabric, causing mildew stains. A single or double mat will hold glass away from fabric.

Stitch Guide

BASIC STITCHERY

CROSS-STITCH (x): There are two ways of making a basic Cross-Stitch. The first method is used when working rows of stitches in the same color. The first step makes the bottom half of the stitches across the row, and the second step makes the top half.

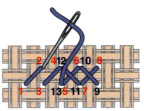

The second method is used when making single stitches. The bottom and top halves of each stitch are worked before starting the next stitch.

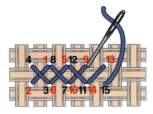

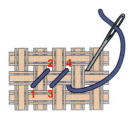

HALF CROSS-STITCH (½x): The first part of a Cross-Stitch. May slant in either direction.

QUARTER CROSS-STITCH (¼x): Stitch may slant in any direction.

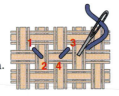

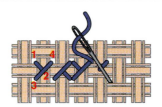

THREE-QUARTER CROSS-STITCH (¾x): A Half Cross-Stitch plus a Quarter Cross-Stitch. May slant in any direction.

HERRINGBONE STITCH

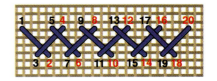

BULLION STITCH

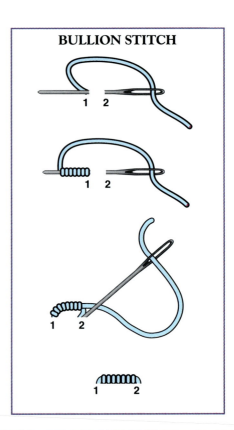

EMBELLISHING WITH EMBROIDERY

EMBROIDERY stitches add detail and dimension to stitching. Unless otherwise noted, work Backstitches first, then other embroidery stitches.

BACKSTITCH   **FRENCH KNOT**   **LAZY DAISY**   **STRAIGHT STITCH**

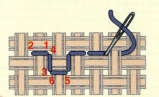   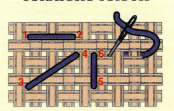

Acknowledgments

We would like to express our appreciation to the many people who helped create this book. Our special thanks go to each of the talented designers who contributed original designs and to our extraordinary models: Robin Gilliam, Keith and Micah Godfrey, who patiently posed for each photograph.

The beautiful photography locations in Texas were provided by James and Mary Barnett, Arp; Kepen and Robin Gilliam, Chapel Hill; Charlotte Stevens, Sunday House, Mineola.

A special thanks to Broadway Florist, Big Sandy; Bill Whitaker, Tyler, for supplying our wonderful photography props and The Frame Up Galley, Tyler, for the beautiful framing.

Our sincerest thanks and appreciation goes to the following manufacturers for generously providing their products for use in the following projects:

BUCILLA®
Needlework Card: Perfect Pansies

CHARLES CRAFT, INC.
Aida: Basket of Apples; God's Garden; Happy Home Recipe; Holiday Trims
Fiddler's Lite®: Country Ornaments
KitchenMates™ Pot Holder & Huck Towel: Garden Kitchen Set
Monaco: Circle of Roses; Enchanted Castle; Santa; Seasonal Birds
Waste Canvas: Fishing Buddies

DANIEL ENTERPRISES
Crafter's Pride Golf Hat: Fishing Buddies

DMC®
Embroidery Floss: A Mother's Love; Angels; Basket of Apples; Beauty Blooms; Christmas Bear; Circle of Roses; Country Ornaments; Elegant Ornaments; Enchanted Castle; First of May; Fishing Buddies; Garden Kitchen Set; God's Garden; Happy Home Recipe; Indigo; Kitty With Flowers; Marriage Sampler; Mr. Snowman; Old Fashioned Flower Basket; Orchid & Butterfly; Perfect Pansies; Santa; Santa's Cat; Seasonal Birds; Simple Pleasures; Spring Bouquets; Sweet Friendships; Teacups; To Have Friends
Metallic Thread: Marriage Sampler
Rayon Floss: Indigo

FAIRFIELD PROCESSING CORP.
Batting: Beauty Blooms; Santa
Soft Touch® Pillow Form: Angels; Circle of Roses; First of May; Rose Heart

KREINIK
Blending Filament: First of May; Marriage Sampler
Fine (#8) Braid: Marriage Sampler; Rose Heart

MADEIRA
Decora Floss: Rose Heart; Unicorn Sampler
Silk Floss: Rose Heart

MILL HILL
Seed Beads: Holiday Trims; Perfect Pansies

NOVTEX
Decorative Trim: Santa

OFFRAY
Miniature Roses: For Wrent

PUTNAM SOFT SHAPES
Batting: Holiday Trims

RHODE ISLAND TEXTILES
RibbonFloss™: Holiday Trims

SUDBERRY HOUSE
Small Tea Tray: Sweet Friendships

WICHELT IMPORTS, INC.
Wooden Bell Pull: A Mother's Love
Brass Bell Pull: Perfect Pansies
Linen: Christmas Bear; Perfect Pansies; Teacups
Jobelan®: Orchid & Butterfly; Simple Pleasures

WRIGHTS®
Lace: Perfect Pansies

ZWEIGART®
Aida: Advice to the Graduate; Mr. Snowman; To Have Friends; Unicorn Sampler
Annabelle®: First of May
Cashel Linen®: Old Fashioned Flower Basket
Lincoln: Sweet Friendships
Lugana®: Angels; Kitty With Flowers; Santa's Cat; Spring Bouquets
Meran: Indigo
Pastel Linen: Beauty Blooms
Quaker Cloth®: Elegant Ornaments
Stitchband: A Mother's Love
Yorkshire Aida: Rose Heart

Pattern Index

A Mother's Love, 70
A True Friend, 68
Advice to the Graduate, 116
Angels, 122

Basket of Apples, 11
Beauty Blooms, 74
Believing, 98
Best Friends, 66

Christmas Bear, 135
Circle of Roses, 40
Consider the Birds, 113
Country Ornaments, 132

Elegant Ornaments, 129
Enchanted Castle, 48

First of May, 106
Fishing Buddies, 60
Flying Angel, 149

For Wrent, 86

Garden Alphabet, 94
Garden Kitchen Set, 17
God's Garden, 91

Happy Home Recipe, 8
Help Me Remember, 110
Holiday Trims, 126

Indigo, 77

Kitty With Flowers, 14

Let Love, 102

Marriage Sampler, 44
Mr. Snowman, 146

Old Fashioned Flower Basket, 35
Orchid & Butterfly, 38

Pastry Shop, 20
Perfect Pansies, 80
Plant a Garden, 88

Rose Heart, 63

Santa, 142
Santa's Cat, 138
Seasonal Birds, 28
Simple Pleasures, 104
Spring Bouquets, 83
Sweet Friendships, 54

Teacups, 24
To Have Friends, 56

Unicorn Sampler, 32

Designer Index

Chrispens, Judith M., 35, 104
Coroso, Marsha J., 110

Davis, Brenda, 44
Davis, Dianne, 11

Fox, Jacquelyn, 54, 60, 74, 83

Harman, Bennie, 102
Hendricks, Christine, 88
Hurley, Kathleen, 8, 14, 40, 91

Kellogg, Pamela, 77, 138

Lange, Celia, 126

Michael, Ursula, 70, 80, 106

Pettersen, Monika, 66

Quinn, Linda, 132, 146

Reed, Thomas, 68

Smith, Barbara, 20

Stedry, Dayna, 86, 94, 149

Vickery, Mike, 17, 24, 28, 38, 48, 56, 122, 129, 135, 142

Williams, Felicia L., 32, 113
Wolf, Linda Moore, 63, 116

Zednick, Tina, 98